*You have been*

# Chosen for
# THIS
## Assignment

*Eunice Woods Cohee*

Chosen For THIS Assignment

ISBN: *9798853962804* (Paperback)

*MeGriHam* Publishing

Printed in the United States of America

# CHOSEN FOR *THIS* ASSIGNMENT

## CONTENTS

*I am deeply indebted to the editors, Corrie M. Anders and Cheryl Jeffries, for their constructive feedback, careful editing and timely handling of my manuscript.*

## SPECIAL ACKNOWLEDGEMENT

*I am a retired English teacher so I thought writing and publishing my first book would be easy, but it was harder than I thought and more rewarding than I could have ever imagined. None of this would have been possible without the constant encouragement and ever-patient support of my publishing company CEO, Melanie of Megriham Publishing. Without her, I may have given up. I know she was sent by God to help me fulfill my assignment, and she did it with great expertise, class and wisdom, never complaining to me about any of the setbacks nor delays that "I" caused. She is a "true servant of God." May The Lord bless you abundantly, Melanie, and increase your entrepreneurial territories.*

*Eunice Anders Woods Cohee* is a Spirit-filled ordained minister of the gospel and a retired high school teacher. She attended North Carolina Central University and Virginia State University, obtaining both her bachelor's and master's degrees from Virginia State.

In 2020 the Lord birthed within her the EUNICE WOODS COHEE MINISTRIES, and in 2021 the vision of spreading the Gospel on a greater online social media ministry became a reality and is addressed on her website, *eunicewoodscoheeministries.com*

Her ministry can be seen on Facebook Live, YouTube and Instagram on her broadcasts, LUNCHING ON THE WORD, POP-IN PRAYER & PRAISE and GOOD NEWS BIBLE STORY TIME.

But 20 years before the birthing of the Eunice Woods Cohee Ministries, The Lord had impregnated her with the seed of this book that you now hold. The seed became actual words on paper that flowed until one day, the flow stopped. It became clear to her that she could not resume writing until God began to speak again and until she had begun to walk more fully in the pathway of the assignment. Later, procrastination and busyness stopped her until finally, The Lord impressed upon her that it was time to complete the book.

Pastor "E," as she is affectionately called by some, is the daughter of the late Pastor Corrie and First Lady Gertrude Anders, the founders of New Bethel Pentecostal Holiness Church, (now known as Bethel Christian Assembly in

Fayetteville, NC, pastored by Bishop Jerry and First Lady Frances Swinney).

She is thankful for her husband, Bro. Robert Cohee, her blended family of six adult children and their spouses, six grandchildren and grandson-in-law, two great-grandchildren and her siblings.

In her spare time she enjoys reading, traveling stateside and abroad and hanging out with her nuclear and extended family.

# *Dedication*

This book is dedicated to the Lord Jesus Christ for His faithfulness and patience with me in moving forward in my assignment. I am so glad and so thankful that He called me and chose me to do His bidding although I didn't feel qualified. But He equipped me, anointed me and called me out from among the ranks of my peers and established my feet on the path of ministry and servanthood.

This book is also dedicated to my mother and father, the late Pastor and First Lady Corrie and Gertrude Anders, who were huge supporters of the call of God on my life. They instilled in me a passion for serving the Lord and being steadfast in Him regardless of obstacles sent to deter me from my destiny.

Next, this book is dedicated to my beloved sister, Hazel Anders Lucas, who was working as one of the editors of my book, when she passed unexpectedly. I salute her and my eldest brother, Corrie Anders, who picked up the reins from Hazel and continued and finished the editing process. Thank you, Corrie. This book is also dedicated to my other two wonderful siblings, Carolyn Anders and Mary Anders, who have been strong supporters. To my siblings and to the memory of my brother, Stephen Anders, I love you all so much! You're the Best!!

Finally, I dedicate this to my two children, Percy Woods, Jr, a minister and high school business teacher and to my daughter, Yemana Woods Dove, a Christian fiction writer. Both of them, who lived through some of the most challenging days of my life, stood by me, supported and encouraged me to the highest degree. They witnessed also the days of triumph and rejoiced with me. I couldn't have asked for better children - I love you two very much!

# ACKNOWLEDGEMENTS

*I am grateful that I was blessed with these people in my life.*

1. The late Bishop Joan Sanders who spoke LIFE into me and strengthened my faith with the Word.

2. The late Bishop Samuel Wright, Sr. who walked me through the dark days and led me as a good shepherd leads his sheep.

3. Paulette Foster who, for 30 years, has poured into my life reminding me that God had a purpose for my life and that I was created for Greater.

4. Special intercessors/friends who covered me in prayer, spoke into my life and who allowed me to cry and question, who gave me the space to just be me: Wanda Owens, Pam Joyner, Frances Swinney, Louise Goings and Bishop Jerry Swinney.

5. Members of Ishi Pentecostal Temple for their love, support and prayers

6. Bishop Richard and Lady Arlene Young for their love, support, and acceptance of my first assignment

7. Bishop Charles H Ellis III who saw potential in me, had faith in my abilities and promoted me within our organization. First Lady Crisette Ellis for her love and support.

8. Marviette Usher who gave me that final push of encouragement to finish this book

9. And I acknowledge all who gave me a platform to preach, teach, minister, counsel, and mentor people of all age groups.

## THANK YOU FOR BELIEVING IN ME!

# FOREWORD

I've had the honor of being under Eunice Cohee's teachings from birth. As her daughter, I can testify that she is an anointed woman of God with a passion for helping others see and understand the gifts that God placed in them. I've seen her, through the grace of God, embrace floundering young people who felt they had no purpose and turn those same young people into a generation hungry for God. Through her life and testimony, insecure and dejected women have been transformed into bold, purpose-driven women of God. Men, unsure of their Godly assignments, have been pushed into a place of confidence beyond what they'd even imagined.

It is a critical hour as we await our soon coming King and now is not the time to back down from what God has called each of us to do. It's time to move! So hold on to your seats because this book is going to stir something in you, it's going to challenge you and it's going to push you to go after God like never before and execute your assignment!


*Yemana Woods Dove*

# *Preface*

"Don't confuse your calling with your assignment.

You're called to fulfill God's purpose.

You're assigned to Specific tasks for God's purpose."

*Unknown*

If God called you

to a task,

He will qualify you

for the job.

*Jack Hyles*

# 1

## ~ YOU'RE GOD'S CHOICE ~

You're "it!" Yes, you, the one who is reading this book. You are God's choice. You are the one that He has chosen for "this" specific assignment, for "this" season and for "this" generation.

I am sure that you are wondering how that came to be. You may be wondering, "What is this assignment?" "Why would God choose me?" "And when did he choose me?" Think back - you have felt a stirring inside you for some time now, but perhaps you have not known that it was God calling you. You may be like the boy Samuel who was aroused by God and heard God calling but did not recognize His voice. It took him running to Eli, the priest, three times before Eli told him, "If he call thee . . . thou shalt say, 'Speak Lord; for Thy servant heareth'" (I Samuel 3:7-10).

But God had called Samuel way before then, just like He called you a long time ago. My friend, it all began before you were even born. In fact, it happened in the Spirit realm before the foundation of the world was created

(Ephesians 1:4a). See, you were in God's mind and in His plan before He created the sun, the moon or the stars. You were in His mind before the dividing of the firmaments to create seas and dry land, before the first animal was created, even before there was an Adam and Eve. God's plan to save lost humanity originated even before man fell into sin. And God's plan to have you help in the rescue started, too, before man fell.

God knew before He created mankind that man would be ensnared and deceived by the tempter, Satan. He knew that man would have to be delivered out of this bondage and be redeemed. He knew also that on the earth He would find no perfect, qualified human redeemer. The only perfect Redeemer would be Himself; therefore, He knew that He would have to wrap Himself in flesh, be born of a virgin, give His life as ransom for the penalty of death that had to be paid – all before He created man. And The Lord knew that after He finished His redemptive work and returned to Glory, that He would need witnesses on this earth to reveal His ultimate display of sacrificial love and to show mankind the route back to Him. So, in His infinite wisdom, God handpicked those witnesses that He knew would fulfill the mission of recruiting lost souls (1 Peter 2:9).

*And knowing that you would have a tender heart toward*
*Him, and knowing your make-up, He chose you!*

He did not choose you based on your merits, your talents, your strength, your good looks, your business or political connections.  He singled you out because He loves you and knew that through you, He would receive glory and honor and that you would help to fulfill His purpose. Actually, on your own merits, you are not smart enough, wise enough, able enough, strong enough, good-looking enough, skilled enough, nor savvy enough to do His good pleasure or His will without Him first extending you the grace to do it.  Remember what He said to Israel when He chose her to be His special people:

*"The Lord did not set His love upon you, nor choose you,*
*because ye were more in number than any people; for ye*
*were the fewest of all people" (Deuteronomy 7:7).*

They were not chosen because God was impressed with their numbers – they had no great numbers with which to impress God.  God has not chosen anyone because they are so great – not Mary, the mother of Jesus; not Deborah, the wise and fearless judge; not Abraham and Sarah, who conceived and brought forth in old age a great nation; not Paul, the great apostle; not Dorcas, the selfless missionary who was full of good works; nor David, the man after God's own heart. None of these were chosen for their greatness; nor was I, nor are you. We are all chosen because God is great and because God is good and because God looked out on us, knew us, extended His grace and said, "I want to use him; I want to use her." I want to use their hands, their mouths, their feet, their gifts (1 Peter 4:10-11).

You may ponder, "Well, if God really knew me, wouldn't He know that I'm not perfect? Wouldn't He know that I mess up from time to time?" The answer is yes, He knows that you are not perfect. Yes, He knows that the chosen do fail sometimes, but your imperfections do not negate nor void His plans for you.

Look at David. He is picked on a lot for his failures. How many times have you heard the story of his adulterous affair with Bathsheba? Yet, he was chosen to rule over Israel, God's people. And what about his murderous plot to have Bathsheba's husband killed to cover up his affair and her subsequent pregnancy?

But God's grace reached out to David. Grace gave him a space to repent. New mercies were extended to him when he cried out earnestly in Psalm 51:1,

*"Have mercy upon me, O God, according to Thy loving-kindness: according unto the multitude of Thy tender mercies, blot out my transgressions."*

David acknowledged that he had failed God and because of his broken spirit and his contrite heart, God forgave him and gave him another chance. This second chance afforded David the privilege of serving God as king over His people, as a mighty warrior against the enemies of Israel and as an anointed psalmist whose words of exaltation, 3000 years later, still minister to the heart of God.

*And you, too, are still chosen by God.*

If you have failed God in the past, go ahead and feel remorse. And know that if you repent, if you turn away from continuing in sin, that God can and will still use you. Remember God knew you and what your failings would be long before you entered the world. And yet you are still in His plan – if you want to be. Rest assured that as you grow in Christ, you will mature in Him and become the holy vessel that He can use. God knows that where you are now in your spiritual walk is not where you are going to end up. Know that God can use you in each stage of your growth or maturity. It is as one noted preacher said recently, "God can use you while He changes you, as long as you are willing, available and still teachable." What an awesome and merciful God we serve!

# 2

## ~ SEPARATED FOR SERVICE ~

God's grace doesn't select you because of your age. In fact, in Jesus' Name, we declare that your age will not be a deterrent in fulfilling the Kingdom work of the Lord. God does not discriminate against any because of age – you can be used by God whether you are young or old, whether you are from the generations called "The Silent Generation," "The Baby Boomers," "Generation X," "Millennials," "Generation Z," or the youngest of them all, "Generation Alpha."

Grace chose Samuel when he was just 12 years old to be a prophet, priest and judge – three major assignments for one that some might think was too young. But in God's viewpoint, Samuel was not too young. Neither did He think Josiah was too young. Grace chose Josiah when he was only eight years old to be the next king of Judah following the assassination of his father, King Amon. Grace chose Jeremiah when he was 17 to be a major prophet. So you see, God uses young people of various ages. He grooms them, matures them and equips them for their assignments.

And God also uses older people who may sometimes feel that their season of usability is over. But if you proclaim, "I'm available Lord," then God can still use you, whether you are in the summer of your life, the fall of your life, or in the winter season of your life. As the children of Israel were about to be allotted and then possess portions of the Promised Land, Caleb stood up at the age of 85 and said to Joshua, "Now give me this mountain (hilly country of Hebron where the Anakite giants lived) that the Lord promised me that day" (Joshua 14:12-15). In other words, Caleb was declaring that I'm still able to be used by God to battle my enemies and possess my land. My age does not dictate what I can and cannot do for the Lord. Whatever God has promised me, I am still able to obtain it. And at 85, Caleb did just that!

God also chose Abraham, another person whom many would consider "over the hill," but when he was 75 years old and childless, God called him to be the father of a nation and the "father of faith." When Abraham thought that he and his wife, Sarah, were too old to be "birthing greatness," they found out that God doesn't let age get in the way of His purpose. The Scriptures inform us that their age didn't hinder God. And it didn't limit their service nor usability to God. In fact, to prove it, God had them wait 25 years before the promise of a child manifested itself; at 100 and 90 years old Abraham and Sarah brought Isaac into the world and discovered that age is just a number with God. God uses whomever He wants, at whatever stages of their lives that He so desires. Age does not deter nor limit God!

And God calls *you* now, the reader of this book, at this time in your life, whether you are a young, middle-aged, older or elderly person. You are of great value to God. And God has need of you at this time and during this season. He calls you and bestows upon you the honor and the distinction of bringing Him glory. He speaks to you now, as He spoke to Jeremiah, the prophet, that before you were born, I sanctified you. In other words,

> *"I separated and set you apart, consecrating you for My service" (Jer. 1:5).*

That's why before you received Jesus, you found it difficult to fit in with the crowd. You tried desperately to fit in. You tried to do whatever your friends did. You tried to be a clone of them. But even when you were out there doing the worldly things, you never felt completely satisfied nor happy. You tried hard to fit in, but you never actually felt like you really belonged. Even your friends knew you were different, that you weren't really one of them. They didn't understand the words, "separated" and "consecrated," but they knew you were different.

That's why when my then-teenaged unsaved son was about to take a drink, his friends stopped him. When he was about to try drugs, his friends said, "No." When he and his friends were harassed by some gang members who subsequently started shooting at them, he grabbed a friend's gun and was about to retaliate, but his friends quickly said, "No, man, that's not you." Although he tried to fit in, his friends already saw what he was trying not to see – that he was already chosen and separated by God before I even gave birth to him. It was in God's mind to use my son for His service as a preacher and teacher. Believe me, it is in God's mind to use you, too.

He has set you apart for a particular work, a particular ministry. Let's look at Moses who was separated and set aside from his fellow Jewish brethren for a particular assignment. What did his separation call for? It called for a disconnection from his family, a disconnection from his culture and a disconnection from the familiar.

To begin with, Moses was separated from his birth parents in order to save his life. A horrible decree had come down from a frightened Pharaoh, the ruler of Egypt, who felt threatened by the exponential growth of the Hebrew people, fearing that one day they might become a military foe. To thwart their growth, he "charged all his people, saying, Every son that is born, ye shall cast into the river, and every daughter ye shall save alive" (Exodus 1:22). Moses' mother hid her son for three months from the would-be murderers until she could hide him no longer. She then made an ark or a sturdily built basket of bulrushes covered with slime and pitch, put him in the basket and placed him at the edge of the river where the Egyptians usually gathered. She disconnected herself from his life in hopes that someone would find him and have compassion on him. And so it happened, by the providence of God, that the daughter of Pharaoh found him, kept him and raised him as her child (Exodus 2:2-10).

It's amazing that Moses did not die, but God had special plans for him. God set him aside, in the enemy's camp, ON PURPOSE, so that he would learn the ways of the Egyptians, learn the culture of the higher echelon and learn how to be comfortable in that atmosphere. His purpose dictated that he would one day need all of that knowledge to fulfill his assignment of delivering God's chosen people, the Israelites, out of Egyptian bondage and slavery.

Have you ever wondered why God let some of you be set apart to live with a family other than your birth parents? For some of you, it was a tragedy. For others, it appeared to be a tragedy, but in retrospect, you look back and see the hand of God in it. You see that God brought you out of a dysfunctional family in order to set you up with one that would bring structure, balance and discipline in your life – ingredients that would be sorely needed for the divine assignment that He had in store for you. But even if you lived life in a dysfunctional family, God still took care of you and turned your pain into a passionate pursuit of knowing His will and plan for your life. Sometimes people are angry at birth parents who gave them up for adoption or sent them to live with other relatives or to foster homes. But consider that many of them did that because they couldn't give you what you needed for the assignment that lay before you. Yes, they set you aside and while it was painful, God used that time to plant seeds of greatness in you that He would later use for His glory.

God planted seeds of greatness in Moses and after living 40 years as an Egyptian prince, circumstances disconnected him from his royal family and sent him to the backside of the Midian desert for a season. (Exodus 2:11-15)

Why the desert? It was because Moses needed a season to prepare for his assignment. For the second 40 years of his life, Moses lived in the desert as a shepherd with his wife, children and father-in-law. For 40 years he learned many lessons from the sheep, the desert, his family and from the Voice of God. He was disconnected from the familiar, from his cultural upbringing, from the easy lifestyle of comfort. But he would need all of the life lessons that he was obtaining in the desert for the assignment that was before him.

We, too, go through a desert/wilderness experience where we sometimes have to forfeit the familiar and the comforts of life, the comfort of marriage, the security of careers, the companionship of friends … all to prepare us to fulfill the assignment of God to deliver His people out of the various bondages in which they are held. As my former pastor, Bishop Samuel Wright, Sr. of Petersburg, VA, once told me, "Preparation Precedes Readiness." God doesn't want to send you out without the necessary readiness. Often, the desert experience is fraught with bittersweet experiences, but don't get angry at God. It's a God Move!

And it will all work out for good and for the fulfilling of your purpose. Trust me, I know. But, more about that later.

Another person set aside from the familiar was Samuel. As a young child, his mother consecrated and dedicated him to serve the Lord. His mother, Hannah, had been barren for many years, and she had sought God earnestly to open her womb. When God answered her prayers, she vowed to nurture the child for three to four years, wean him and then give him to the Lord as a thank you offering. Samuel left the familiarity of a two-parent, Godly home to become the spokesman and judge for God. Was it easy to leave his home? I dare say not. But the purpose of God was so great, the assignment so meaningful that when God chose him and singled him out, it was rather difficult to tell him No, so his answer became "Yes, Lord."

Even Jesus had to submit to the purpose of His life and be cut off from a normal life, from a life of pursuing His own course or destiny. As Jesus grew into manhood, He, too, was disconnected from childhood friends, from His familiar surroundings and even from His family, for He said in one passage of Scripture, "Who is my mother? And who are my brethren?" (Matthew 12:48). He had been sent to the earth and although He loved His family, He had been set apart from them, for His mission in life was different from theirs. His mission was to minister salvation, healings and deliverance to the oppressed. He was not walking the same road as His family and friends. His agenda was totally different from theirs. And so is God's agenda for you – it is different from your friends and family. That is why God sometimes allows a separation to come between you and friends, you and co-workers, you and your employer, you and your family members – He must get you off to yourself – alone – where He can talk to you and with you; where He will be number one in your life and in your thoughts and where your greatest desire will be to please Him and not man.

# Chapter

# 3

## ~ ANOINTED, BUT BROKEN ~

Some of you may ask, but what happens when your desire *is* to please God and you know that you've been anointed for the assignment, but you are broken on the inside?  It is a very unfortunate thing that some of the ones whom God has called and chosen have been damaged by the enemy who saw their potential to impact the Kingdom. Satan, therefore, sought to destroy them before they could make that advance into enemy territory and tear the kingdom of darkness down.  He piled shame and guilt upon them. Let's look at a few that this happened to, but let me warn you now that this does not have to be the ending to your story.

In 1st Samuel 13, we learn the horrific story of a brother raping his half-sister.  This sister, Tamar, is royalty – she is King David's daughter.  Her brother, Amnon, has become infatuated with her and desires to fulfill his lustful fantasies on her.  Proclaiming that he loves her, he yearns for her. Taking the advice of a relative, he makes himself sick and then asks King David if Tamar could bring him some food.

David and Tamar, both unsuspecting of Amnon's real motive, consent and she prepares the food for him and takes it to him where she is then roughly handled and raped. When his lust has been spent, he is then repulsed by her and orders his servant to drag her away from his sight. She begs him not to send her away in such disgrace, for her reputation would be ruined and she feels that she would be no good to anyone. As is usually the case, the victim takes the shame, the blame and the guilt that Amnon, the perpetrator should have taken. This royal daughter, who was destined to carry greatness in her, instead bears unforgettable shame. No one comes to her rescue. No one counsels her. No one stands up for her. No one gives her beauty for her ashes. No one tells her that although she has been abused, she is still beautiful in the sight of God and in the sight of her family. No one tells her that she is still a woman of value and honor. Rather, everyone who knows about the tragic incident allows her to live the rest of her life, hidden away from society, feeling useless and unworthy. Instead of her healing and singing the songs of praise that her father had penned years earlier, she sinks down in despair – and never recovers. She was a chosen vessel of God who was marred by sexual abuse and a resulting low sense of self-worth.

Too many times this is happening in our world today – we are wounding our brothers and sisters. We are bruising the very ones that Christ was bruised for on Calvary, the very ones that He died for and carried their infirmities and pain so that they would not have to. And so, here we are in the 21st century, yet piercing and bruising God's Called Out ones, His Anointed Vessels. And here are our brothers and sisters, wandering around bewildered and confused, carrying the weight of their abuses, fears, shame and hurts, too heavy laden to go forth in full magnitude and power in the things that God has chosen to do through them.

You might know someone or you may be one of those anointed people who has been abused sexually, physically, emotionally or verbally. The calling on your life is unmistakable and people push you to go forward and use your gifts, to flow in the anointing, but you ask, "Lord, how can I flow, how can I be used by You when I am so broken and scarred by these negative experiences that deep down I don't feel worthy to be used by You?" "How can I sing for You? How can I teach or preach Your Word? How can I reach the lost for you? How can I use these creative gifts You gave me? How can I empower others? How can I exercise the gifts You gave me when I'm sick myself and tortured by the thoughts, dreams and nightmares of the one(s) who victimized me in my youth and adult years with their lust, their rage, their physical blows, their evil threatenings, their belittling putdowns and even with their parental absenteeism in my life ?"

Let me assure you that the devil cannot snuff out what God has put in you. Yes, your pain is real. Your trauma from the experiences is real. Your hurt is undeniably real. You have been through what no person should ever have to go through. The enemy meant for all of the abuses to break you down so low that you would never have the strength nor desire to lift your head again. He meant to destroy the anointing God placed on you and the ministry gifts in you. Why? Because you are a threat to the enemy's kingdom of darkness! Some people have been under heavy attack and have never recovered from it. But you, my brother, and you, my sister, you cannot be silenced! Your voice has to be heard for it is a voice to be reckoned with. You, my brother and sister, must survive the storms you've been through. You must heal from the inside out. You must not only survive, but you must thrive. You must rebound. You must live! You must live again! You must, therefore, be healed!! Chosen vessel, you must be made whole, and so, I therefore pray and speak the name of Jesus Christ into your yesterday's pains and into your today's hurts.

According to the word of the Lord in Jeremiah 30:17 and Luke 4:18, I declare and decree healing in THE NAME OF JESUS CHRIST to every wound that you have suffered in your childhood and adulthood. Lord, remove the stigma, heal the hurts, perform internal surgery on the anger and unforgiveness. Cut them out from the root. Cut out self-hatred. In the name of Jesus, I cut out the lying words from your memory that were spoken over you. I cut out the low self-worth and speak a healthy sense of identity in you.

In the Name of Jesus, I send The Word of healing to each of you and declare that God is delivering you from every destructive act that targeted you (Psalm 107:20). I send this word to matriculate in your spirit, that God is your saving strength (Psalm 28:8) and He is the lifter up of your head from all shame and pain (Psalm 3:3).

In the Name of Jesus Christ, I set you free from your painful past. I set you free from the bad memories. I set you free from your yesterday's tragedies. I declare in Jesus' Name that you are loosed from all your infirmities (Luke 13:11-12).

And I pray for your children, your children's children, both present and those to come, and I declare that this generational cycle ends NOW. I pray that you who were formerly broken will speak over your seed and break that damaging cycle of abuse.

I speak "wholeness" into your spirit man, wholeness into your emotions, and wholeness into your thinking – no more faulty thinking.

Spirit of the Living God, stand up mightily in this vessel of yours and in their seed until all mental and emotional brokenness is gone and is replaced by your healing, deliverance and wholeness. Now say aloud and emphatically, "Lord, I receive my healing; I receive my deliverance; I receive my freedom from what used to torment me. I receive my wholeness." Now open your eyes and see yourself as Christ sees you, as Free!

Chosen vessel, I command your eyes to open in the Name of Jesus to witness your *full* beauty, full worth, full value, and full inner healing. *And to any lingering doubt that you may be harboring, I say to you, yes, you ARE deeply loved by The Lord.* Rehearse that repeatedly in your mind. You are the apple of His eye, meaning He cherishes and loves you very much.

And yes, He wants to use you! How you may ask? As deliverers, using your own experiences, to help so many other people who are still broken, still distraught, still captive to negative emotions and thoughts. The Lord needs YOU to set these captives free – it may be done through the lyrics you write, the songs you sing, the prayer intercession you offer, the words in the books that you author, the dreams/visions He gives you, the wise counseling you give, the fatherly/motherly figure you portray to ones in need of such or the healing and deliverance ministry that He has given you. It may be done through you, the preacher, the educator, the professional, the entrepreneur. In every area, in every field there is a person waiting on YOU to set them free by the power of Jesus Christ. They stand ready to be put back together again. This, my friend, is your new reality – a WHOLE you, chosen to help bring others into this same state of wholeness.

# 4

## ~ FLAWED, BUT STILL CHOSEN ~

The last chapter spoke of broken people; this chapter speaks to all who claim that they can't be used by God because they aren't perfect and it speaks to those who feel they are perfect enough as is . . .

Understand this – we all have character defects!  And guess what?  Your God knew this when He created you. He knew that you were "marred clay" (in other words, imperfect) and yet He insisted that you come forth into the earth realm to carry out the assignment He had prepared for you. It's YOUR assignment, defects and all. This does not mean that God wants you to be content with your deficiencies; it is His desire that you develop into the mature son or daughter that can be used without destroying your destiny.

Such was the case with Moses. He was called from his mother's womb - that's why God went through great lengths to save him from certain death and preserve him for his future undertaking.

At age 40, Moses thought he was ready - he felt the call of a deliverer on his life, but he had not yet fully developed into the chosen vessel that God could use unabashedly and unreservedly. Prematurely, Moses stepped out, in fury, as a deliverer to rescue a fellow Hebrew out of the hands of a violent Egyptian. He killed the Egyptian and buried him. The next day when two Hebrew men got into an altercation, Moses stepped in again as a would-be deliverer and tried to adjudicate the matter. The Hebrew who was guilty of instigating the fight cried out,

> *"Who made thee a prince and a judge over us? Intendest thou to kill me as thou killedst the Egyptian? And Moses feared, and said, Surely this thing is known. Now when Pharaoh heard this thing, he sought to slay Moses. But Moses fled from the face of Pharaoh, and dwelt in the land of Midian..." (Exodus 2:14-15)*

Though the hand of God was upon Moses and although his destiny entailed being a deliverer for his people, it was not yet his season to be sent out to fulfill it. That happens far too often in the church today with people who have a calling as ministers, musicians, psalmists, prophets...

We can learn a lot from David, the young shepherd, who had several great callings on his life as did Moses. But notice the difference in how David sought to fulfill his calling. David stayed in the background in the hills and valleys with the sheep while he perfected his music craft. He spent time alone with God talking to God and letting God speak to him. He allowed God to teach him and minister to him the valuable lessons he would need to fulfill his assignment. Out of these experiences came a great anointing on David, an anointing to worship God through penning lyrics to song/psalms, to worship God through the flow of music he composed, to worship God through the skillful playing of the harp and to value His word and guidance. He learned to wait patiently on God. All of this he learned BEFORE being requested to go into King Saul's court to play therapeutic music that would drive out the evil spirits that tormented Saul (1 Samuel 16:14-23). If he had gone too soon into the "music ministry" without proper teaching, solitude with God and a solid Godly base under him, David could have been devoured, ensnared, and trapped by those same evil spirits that beset Saul.

All who are called today and given an assignment by God should take the time to go through the spiritual maturation process. Yes, you are gifted and it's evident. But don't let people nor your pride in your abilities push you into a destiny for which you're not yet quite ready. "Sit at the feet of Gamaliel" (your leaders) as Paul the Apostle did and learn first. Be patient - your time will come.

Every person called and chosen by God also must be humble enough to know that if you're going to be used by God that it is imperative that you first must know and understand the Word. **The Word is God!** *No matter what your assignment is, you must know the Word and you must spend time alone with God in prayer so that you can get His perspective, His direction, His approval and His say so for when it is time for you to step out.*

Jesus modeled this well for us. Before sending his disciples out to minister, He taught them for about three years. After initially equipping them, He sent the 12 apostles out and later 70 disciples to minister. And even after this, they stayed in ongoing training, being taught even the more for 40 days after Christ's resurrection. The Word of God not only taught them how to minister but also how to eliminate the character flaws. See, God knows you've got those character flaws, but He still wants to use you . . . and He'll do so as He also points out your flaws so that you can correct them.

Paul, the great apostle, thought it necessary to be taught by God; he went to the desert of Arabia to be personally taught by God, to be emboldened by the Word he learned, to have his self-righteous heart of hatred against the Christians turned and transformed into a heart of love where he became "one of them" and sought to bring others into this marvelous light that his own eyes now perceived. He came out of Arabia a changed man, a better man, a man armed with God's Word and its application, a man now, not only called, but anointed, chosen and sent forth. People immediately saw the difference in Paul.

**You want it to be seen that you have been with Jesus!**

*"Now when they saw the boldness of Peter and John, and perceived that they were unlearned and ignorant men, they marvelled; and they took knowledge of them, that they had been with Jesus" (Acts 4:13).*

~~~~~~~~~

**PREPARATION PRECEDES READINESS**. Before you take off on your assignment, let me repeat again - take time to study God's Word and get your feet planted on a solid base of Truth. Learn your craft through what the Bible teaches. Learn the character, the integrity of what it takes to be a fully sold out and yielded vessel. Stay in seclusion for awhile and let God work on your character defects. That's what happened with Moses.

God took Moses to the backside of a desert and honed his character. God worked on him for a third of his life, refining him, humbling him, working on his anger problem...then turning his weaknesses into strengths. See, even the weakness of anger can be retargeted, redirected so that it becomes a holy anger that does not sin. Those are just a few lessons that Moses learned before stepping onto the world's stage as a deliverer. No, it may not take God that long with you - after all, today we don't even have the lifespan that the Old Testament biblical characters had.

Another important lesson is to take the time to learn about the people to whom you will be ministering. To whom are you being sent? And what is your mission as it relates to them? Take time to determine your attitude towards those you will serve. Is your attitude haughty, thinking that you are better than them? Do you have a callous attitude toward them? Or are you tender-hearted and compassionate?

Are you being sent to heal broken-hearted people through the ministry of music or through the ministry of preaching and teaching or through the ministry of counseling and deliverance? Then study the nature of such people through the Word and other resources.

Study the scriptures to see the types of attacks that were sent against people with your type anointing. Study to see their reactions to the assaults and plots. What weapons did they counter with? Malice? Revenge? Compassion?

Stephen, a New Testament deacon, countered with prayer, love and forgiveness when the Jewish people stoned him for preaching the gospel (Acts 7:54-60). Other gifted and chosen vessels also countered with fervent prayer and Word. Although it was a fearful situation, note how the saints and elders prayed after Peter and John had been released from prison after being beaten for preaching the gospel and healing a lame man.

> *"And now, Lord, behold their threatenings: and grant unto thy servants, that with all boldness they may speak thy word, By stretching forth thine hand to heal; and that signs and wonders may be done by the name of thy holy child Jesus. And when they had*

*prayed, the place was shaken where they were assembled together; and they were all filled with the Holy Ghost, and they spake the word of God with boldness." (Acts 4:29-31)*

Prayer cancelled out the fear that had arisen in them. The Lord didn't cancel their assignment nor delete them from His roll of Kingdom workers because of their fear, but He strengthened them and replaced the fear with boldness. That's why it's so important to pray so that God can help you deal with your weaknesses and flaws.

The Lord had to help Peter early in his spiritual walk to correct some flaws, mainly his anger and violent nature. That's why He told Peter to put up his sword.

*"And Jesus said unto him, Friend (Judas), wherefore art thou come? Then came they, and laid hands on Jesus and took him. And, behold, one of them which were with Jesus stretched out his hand, and drew his sword, and struck a servant of the high priest's, and smote off his ear. Then said Jesus unto him, Put up again thy sword into his place: for all they that take the sword shall perish with the sword. Thinkest thou that I cannot now pray to my Father,*

*and he shall presently give me more than twelve*
*legions of angels?" (Matthew 26:50-53)*

I can imagine the Lord telling Peter, "You're not going
to operate with that show of physical power, but you must
learn to operate in the power of the Holy Ghost and
restraint when people lie on you, mistreat you, try to kill
you, stone you... I've got to mold and shape you Peter. I've
got to use my hands to craft that defect out of you."

The Lord had to deal with the flaws also in two other
disciples. He didn't toss them away because of the flaw.
He still used them – after correcting them. He rebuked
James and John for their unrighteous anger when they
wanted to call down fire from Heaven against those who
rejected and humiliated the Lord's attempt to pass through
their city:

> *"And sent messengers before his face: and they*
> *went, and entered into a village of the Samaritans,*
> *to make ready for him. And they did not receive him,*
> *because his face was as though he would go to*
> *Jerusalem. And when his disciples James and John*
> *saw this, they said, Lord, wilt thou that we*
> *command fire to come down from heaven, and*

*consume them, even as Elias did? But he turned,*
*and rebuked them, and said, Ye know not what*
*manner of spirit ye are of. For the Son of man is not*
*come to destroy men's lives, but to save them. And*
*they went to another village." (Luke 9:52-56)*

The same chosen James and John had to be rebuked on another occasion for their **selfish ambition** steeped in pride, as they tried to make a name for themselves.

*"Then came to him the mother of Zebedee's*
*children with her sons, worshipping him, and*
*desiring a certain thing of him. And he said unto*
*her, What wilt thou? She saith unto him, Grant that*
*these my two sons may sit, the one on thy right*
*hand, and the other on the left, in thy kingdom. But*
*Jesus answered and said, Ye know not what ye ask.*
*Are ye able to drink of the cup that I shall drink of,*
*and to be baptized with the baptism that I am*
*baptized with? They say unto him, We are able. And*
*he saith unto them, Ye shall drink indeed of my cup,*
*and be baptized with the baptism that I am baptized*
*with: but to sit on my right hand, and on my left, is*
*not mine to give, but it shall be given to them for*
*whom it is prepared of my Father. And when the ten*

*heard it, they were moved with indignation against the two brethren." (Matthew 20:20-25)*

How often does that spirit of pride and ambition creep into God's anointed ones! We must be constantly on guard against that. If that is a flaw within you, let the Refiner work on you some more so that you can bring that spirit under subjection. He still wants to use you.

# Chapter

## 5

## ~ CHOSEN BUT UNDER PRESSURE ~

Pressure? What is pressure? Pressure is defined by the Merriam-Webster dictionary as "the burden of mental or physical distress especially from grief, illness, or adversity."

And why does it come? Satan uses the pressure of mental or physical distress as a tool to alienate you from your Creator. He uses it to pull you away from your assignment and drag you down into a state of negativity, complaining and bitterness. God, on the other hand, uses pressure to build you up, to mature you to a level where you can handle any situation that is thrown your way and to develop your faith in His power to provide and deliver you. Although pressure is allowed to come your way, understand that God does not leave you alone to deal with that burden, stress, or adversity – He is very much present with you and will cause you to be victorious over the distress – if you don't faint under the weight of the pressure.

The children of Israel had to deal with many situations after leaving Egypt, the place of their former captivity; they initially left gleefully to fulfill their God-given assignment.

But as times got hard, as test after test confronted them, they portrayed for us what NOT to do when under pressure. Let's review their story and consider the assignment that was given to them as recorded by Moses in Exodus 3:16-18; 21-22:

> "Go, and gather the elders of Israel together, and say unto them, The Lord God of your fathers, the God of Abraham, of Isaac, and of Jacob, appeared unto me, saying, I have surely visited you, and seen that which is done to you in Egypt: And I have said, I will bring you up out of the affliction of Egypt unto the land of the Canaanites, and the Hittites, and the Amorites, and the Perizzites, and the Hivites, and the Jebusites, unto a land flowing with milk and honey. And they shall hearken to thy voice: and thou shalt come, thou and the elders of Israel, unto the king of Egypt, and ye shall say unto him, The Lord God of the Hebrews hath met with us: and now let us go, we beseech thee, three days' journey into the wilderness, *that we may sacrifice to the Lord our God.*"

In other words, their assignment was to go into the wilderness and worship the Lord, giving Him sacrifices of praise and honor.

*"And I will give this people favour in the sight of the Egyptians: and it shall come to pass, that, when ye go, ye shall not go empty. But every woman shall borrow of her neighbour, and of her that sojourneth in her house, jewels of silver, and jewels of gold, and raiment: and ye shall put them upon your sons, and upon your daughters; and ye shall spoil the Egyptians." (vs 21-22)*

Moses, speaking as God's ambassador, said to Pharaoh, "Let my people go that they may worship ME in the desert." Notice that there is no mention of going to Canaan, the Promised Land.

After Pharoah and his people suffered through 10 horrific plagues, while Israel suffered through none of them, Pharoah finally relented and let the Israelites leave. But they did not leave empty handed; they left with jewels of silver, jewels of gold, and costly raiment, received from the Egyptians. The Israelites left with things they could use to *worship* in the desert – note again, not in Canaan, The Promised Land, but in the desert and wilderness.

True enough, their ultimate destination would be The

Promised Land, but their first assignment had to be fulfilled in the wilderness/desert. What was their assignment again? It was to worship God, not in a luscious, thriving location, but in the wilderness, in a desolate place, an isolated place where God could be encountered in intense experiences that revealed His mighty power which would, in turn, cause the Israelites to glorify God and make known His great deeds. You see, the wilderness experience reveals your need of God and shows His willingness to deliver you in such an awesome manner that you can't help but praise God for His mighty acts! But Israel faltered in fulfilling her assignment when the pressures of the wilderness life increased.

Their first big test came when Pharoah decided to follow after the children of Israel and re-enslave them. The Israelites had only gotten as far as the Red Sea and here, they were blocked in. They could go no further for the Red Sea was before them, stopping them from advancing. The mountains were on either side of them, prohibiting them from escaping to the left or to the right. And the dreadful and angry Pharaoh and his large army were behind them, quickly closing in. The Israelites feared their outcome and immediately took out their frightening desperation on

Moses, their leader. Their fear provoked them to lash out and say,

> *"Because there were no graves in Egypt, hast thou taken us away to die in the wilderness? wherefore hast thou dealt thus with us, to carry us forth out of Egypt? Is not this the word that we did tell thee in Egypt, saying, Let us alone, that we may serve the Egyptians? For it had been better for us to serve the Egyptians, than that we should die in the wilderness." (Exodus 14:11-12)*

Was this the response that God was looking for? No, He was looking for a vote of confidence that conveyed that if He had sent them out on a mission, then He would ensure that they were able to accomplish it. He had sent them out to worship Him. Instead, He received their first complaint.

But God, who is so merciful, did not cast them to the side because they failed their first test. Rather, He gave this response through Moses:

> *"Fear ye not, stand still, and see the salvation of the LORD, which he will shew to you to day: for the Egyptians whom ye have seen to day, ye shall see*

*them again no more for ever. The LORD shall fight*
*for you, and ye shall hold your peace" (Exodus*
*14:13-14).*

And God miraculously made the Red Sea to divide and become dry land for the children of Israel to walk upon, unencumbered, and get to the other side. And He defeated and overthrew Pharaoh and his army, jamming their chariot wheels in the sea bed when the waters of the divided sea came crashing back upon them and killed them all.

The children of Israel were beside themselves with joy. Their faith in God intensified and they began to fulfill their assignment of worshipping God. They sang one of the most powerful songs of adoration ever recorded in Exodus 15. They danced in praise. They glorified God! They proclaimed His might! They declared in wonder,

> *"Who is like unto thee, O Lord, among the gods?*
> *who is like thee, glorious in holiness, fearful in*
> *praises, doing wonders? Thou stretchedst out thy*
> *right hand, the earth swallowed them. Thou in thy*
> *mercy hast led forth the people which thou hast*
> *redeemed: thou hast guided them in thy strength*
> *unto thy holy habitation. The people shall hear, and*
> *be afraid: sorrow shall take hold on the inhabitants*

*of Palestina. Then the dukes of Edom shall be amazed; the mighty men of Moab, trembling shall take hold upon them; all the inhabitants of Canaan shall melt away" (vs 11-15).*

### God's chosen people had now given Him what He wanted—worship!

After this great deliverance, their second pressure test led them, *three days later*, to the wilderness of Shur.

> *"So Moses brought Israel from the Red sea, and they went out into the wilderness of Shur; and they went three days in the wilderness, **and found no water.** And when they came to Marah, they could not drink of the waters of Marah, for they were bitter: therefore the name of it was called Marah. And **the people murmured** against Moses, saying, What shall we drink? And he cried unto the LORD; and the LORD shewed him a tree, which when he had cast into the waters, the waters were made sweet: there he made for them a statute and an ordinance, and there he proved (tested) them" (Exodus 15:22-25).*

Did you see what their reactions were? They murmured. When pressure came against them, when lack of water presented itself to them, their response was to complain – again. In three short days, they had forgotten about their assignment and forgotten the great deliverance that God had just performed for them. It's unbelievable that they could forget so quickly. But do I ascertain a lesson in this for us all? Yes, we are chosen by God and He has given each of us an assignment, but these assignments do not come without testing. They do not come without wilderness experiences where too often we let fear rob us of our continued faith in The Lord. But in each wilderness experience, God proves Himself faithful and committed to our deliverance and our growth and development – even as He continued to do for Israel. Although they gave Him no worship, He yet assuaged their thirst and gave them sweet water to drink. On your road to fulfilling your assignments, what are you giving God – worship or complaints?

Israel journeyed onto several other places, to the Wilderness of Sin, where they dealt with a food shortage and there murmured against God again, then onto Rephidim where they lacked water a second time and sharply criticized Moses, uttering words in anger that nearly brought on a mutiny. They questioned God's providence and wisdom, even crying out, "Would to God we had died by the hand of the LORD in the land of Egypt" (Exodus 16:3).

Everywhere they went, they complained if they encountered any type of adversity. And every place they went, they let lack, ingratitude, and faithless attitudes get in their way of fulfilling their assignment. They let misfortunes and difficulties get in their way. Yet, each time God delivered them from their adversities. He showed them repeatedly His mighty hand of power and deliverance. But each time they quickly forgot. They magnified their problems and minimized the power of their God.

Don't follow their example. I repeat, don't follow their example when you get afraid or anxious about a situation. Focusing on the situation or on the problem causes you to take your eyes off of the Master and put it on yourself. It causes you to forget the old song, "Jesus, I'll Never Forget What You've Done for Me." It causes you to forget all of the past deliverances God has brought you through. And what He has brought you through before He is God enough to do again! Think about this -

*Did God suddenly stop being God?*
*Did His power suddenly dry up?*

*Did His right hand of power suddenly weaken?*
*Did His integrity fail?*
*Did His reputation as a faithful God decline?*
*Did His reputation as a Promise Keeper falter?*
*Did He quit being the Almighty God with ALL power in His hands?*

### The answer is an emphatic NO!

There was no need for Israel to worry and complain. They had seen God work on their behalf in Egypt with the 10 plagues that came upon the Egyptians, but that didn't come near them because they were under a BLOOD COVERING of protection!

They had seen God stop their enemy at the Red Sea. So how could they forget so quickly? But the Israelites weren't the only forgetful people.

How quickly we, too, forget the deliverances of the past! How quickly we, too, forget the healings! How quickly we, too, forget the grace of God that is sufficient for our every need! What He did yesterday and in yesteryears for Israel should have been a CONSTANT REMINDER to them and to you and me today that God is able to perform again, in your present and in your future.

His covenant with us still stands, even in the wilderness! Your wilderness experience may take you to low, barren places and to uncomfortable, discouraging, dry and weary places, but you will find that God is also there. He may, at times, be silent as you navigate through your valleys, but He is still there – WITH YOU! He will never leave you to face your storms alone! He does care whether you perish. He does care whether you get to the other side of your storm where the sun is again shining. It has never been God's intent that any of His children should receive a promise from Him and then He not fulfill it.

God gave Israel a promise of Canaan possession and He had Israel on track to receive it just as He has you on track to receive your promise. But first they had to go THROUGH the wilderness; not get stuck in it, but go through it; not wander aimlessly in it but to overcome each adverse situation and move forward into the possession. You, too, must go through the wilderness to arrive at the next dimension of His call on your life. But you can't do it with a negative mindset. You must renew your mind with the Word of God and transform your "woe is me" thinking.

You must renew your mind with God's promise in Numbers 23:19, "God is not a man, that he should lie; neither the son of man, that he should repent: hath he said, and shall he not do it? or hath he spoken, and shall he not make it good?"

Renew your mind with "…Do not be afraid; do not be discouraged, for the Lord your God will be with you wherever you go" (Joshua 1:9b).

Renew your mind with Romans 8:28, "And we know that all things work together for good to them that love God, to them who are the called according to his purpose."

Renew your mind with Philippians 1:6, "Being confident of this very thing, that he which hath begun a good work in you will perform it until the day of Jesus Christ:"

Renew your mind with Galatians 6:9, "And let us not be weary in well doing: for in due season we shall reap, if we faint not."

Renew your mind with the truth from the scriptures that prove that wilderness experiences spiritually strengthen you, establish you in the faith, give you divine revelations and show you the delivering power of God.

Let me call on a few biblical witnesses who can demonstrate what to do and what not to do when you're in a wilderness experience and how to come out of the tests better, not bitter. Let me remind you again that the children of God all have various assignments from God to fulfill; the assignments come with spiritual warfare from the enemy of God. The intense pressures are designed to make you waver in your commitment to fulfilling the assignment, to doubt that "God has your back" and to shut you down, literally. But the pressures will not kill you nor destroy you. Instead, they will strengthen your faith, build and equip you and push you further along in achieving your destiny and purpose.

Paul, the apostle, had Purpose written all over him. He had the favor of God oozing from him. He was filled with so much Kingdom knowledge and revelation that yet today it's mind boggling how much he knew and was able to impart to the body of Christ then and now. There are 27 books in the New Testament; Paul is credited with writing 13 of them. That's almost half of the New Testament! But it came with a cost – it came with pressure.

In 2 Corinthians 11:23-28, 32-33, Paul describes the rough days that he experienced and the intense night difficulties he endured:

> *"[I was] in labours (work) more abundant, in stripes (flogged) above measure, in prisons more frequent, in deaths oft. Of the Jews five times received I forty stripes (lashes) save one. Thrice was I beaten with rods, once was I stoned, thrice I*

*suffered shipwreck, a night and a day I have been in*
*the deep; In journeyings often, in perils of waters,*
*in perils of robbers, in perils by mine own*
*countrymen, in perils by the heathen, in perils in the*
*city, in perils in the wilderness, in perils in the sea,*
*in perils among false brethren; In weariness and*
*painfulness, in watchings (sleepless nights) often, in*
*hunger and thirst, in fastings often, in cold and*
*nakedness. Beside those things that are without, that*
*which cometh upon me daily, the care of all the*
*churches…*

*In Damascus the governor under Aretas the king*
*kept the city of the damascenes with a garrison,*
*desirous to apprehend me: And through a window in*
*a basket was I let down by the wall, and escaped his*
*hands."*

Now a negative mindset won't allow you to worship God under these circumstances because your mind can only think about the horrible injustices you are undergoing. And more than likely, you would question God and ask, "Why are you letting me go through all of this when I'm out here trying to accomplish Your will?" But Paul did not play into the hands of the devil who wanted him to doubt God's goodness and to complain and murmur about "his misfortunes."

Instead Paul admonished us that when we go through our wilderness experiences, to remember that we are the CHOSEN OF GOD with a mandate from Him to maintain a positive, faith outlook that will worship Him – in spite of. I can imagine Paul saying, "I'm under pressure, but I'm also 'under' a mandate to 'be strong and courageous'" (Joshua 1:9); I'm under pressure, but I'm also 'under' a mandate to worship Him with the "sacrifice of praise." In fact, Paul tells us in 1 Thessalonians 5:16, "Rejoice evermore." Then he repeats in Philippians 4:4, **"Rejoice** in the Lord **always**: and again I say, **Rejoice**."

No matter the pressure, Paul's response is don't complain about it but rejoice. Praise God even when you don't feel like it. Bless Him until you do feel like it, until you feel the stirring of joy and strength rise up in you. It is impossible to earnestly praise God and something not happen inside you that changes your outlook, your attitude, and your mindset. Praise to God will stamp out a wilderness negative mindset and push you into your destiny. Anytime you begin to feel weary and depressed about your situation, train your mind to meditate on Philippians 4:8, "Finally, brethren, whatsoever things are true, whatsoever things are honest, whatsoever things are just, whatsoever things are pure, whatsoever things are lovely, whatsoever things are of good report; if there be any virtue, and if there be any praise, think on these things."

Meditate on His Word and then rejoice. I remember once when I was in a very low place and I was filled with despair that brought me to tears and heavy depression. I am known as a praiser and worshipper, but on that particular day I did not feel like praising God. I didn't see my situation changing and I was despondent.

I didn't know then that there was a calling on my life that was pushing me toward something greater in ministry. All I knew was that I was in deep pain. Like the psalmist in Psalm 42, I poured out my heart to God, for "my soul was cast down within me." Minutes ticked by as I sobbed before the Lord. Finally, after a lengthy and sorrowful time with The Lord, I chose to stop lamenting and instead start praising.

The praise did not come out in a rush; it was more like a drip/drop pattern. Slowly a "Lord, I thank You" came out of my mouth. Then another and then another. I began to do like David, who many times started a psalm with sorrow but then before he ended the psalm, would change course as he remembered the track record of God and all that He had delivered him from. He would remember and start giving God praise and thanks. I started praising God more fervently as I, too, remembered. And as I kept reminding myself aloud that "all things work together for good to them that love God, to them who are the called according to his purpose," the praises intensified. My faith arose and I began to "hope…in God." I began to proclaim "for I shall yet praise Him" (Psalm 42:5, 11). I knew God had my back and I knew I was called according to His purpose. Because I knew that somehow everything was going to work together for my good, I got deeper into praise and the tears of sorrow became tears of joy. Oh, I had a hallelujah time with the Lord.

The praise that erupted from me changed my atmosphere, my outlook and my mindset. Oftentimes people would see me and say, "You don't look like what you're going through." It was nothing but the grace of God and His promise to me that kept me.

Do you not know that how you respond to your pressures affects how others see your God? When you respond with praise, believing that God is going to strengthen and deliver you, the world watches. They need a place of refuge. They need a strong Deliverer who hears, sees and acts! When they see you holding it together although hell has broken loose around you, when they don't hear you complaining and murmuring but instead hear you exalting the name of The Lord, then you cause them to turn and investigate this "light" that you are presenting to them. They wonder, "If God can help you maintain joy through your wilderness, then maybe I need to take a second look at Him. Maybe I need to serve Him."

Your worship then becomes an evangelistic tool like it did for Paul and Silas, apostles who were thrown in the deepest recesses of the prison dungeon in Acts 16 for preaching the gospel of Jesus Christ and casting a demon out of a woman. They were imprisoned for doing something good! But neither Paul nor Silas murmured or complained, but the Bible tells us that "at midnight Paul and Silas prayed and sang praises unto God and the prisoners heard them" (vs 25). Notice that the prisoners heard rejoicing, not murmurs and complaints. I say again, they heard rejoicing. What a strange reaction from two men who had just been savagely whipped and had their feet bound in stocks, making movement difficult!

Heaven heard their prayers and praises and caused a great earthquake to occur that shook the foundations of the prison and opened the doors to every prisoner's cell. The prison guard almost took his own life because he felt that all of the prisoners had fled, and his life would have been forfeited had they escaped, but they had not left, not a one.

Normally, prisoners would have fled the scene. But God had a purpose for them staying and for the guard not killing himself. Paul and Silas were *on assignment* to bring salvation to this Philippian jailer. Complaining wouldn't have opened the prison doors, but praise did. And it caused the jailer to ask, "What must I do to be saved?" Salvation came to the jailer and to his household that very night. And liberation from prison came for Paul and Silas. Paul and Silas are great examples for us to emulate when under pressure.

King David is another example of one to emulate, but maybe not in the way that you might think. David had followed The Lord closely most of his life, but there came a time when he let a testing time, a time of temptation, pressure him to take "the forbidden fruit" called Bathsheba and commit adultery with her. Then he had her husband, who was away at war fighting for his country, killed on the battlefield to cover up Bathsheba's subsequent pregnancy. Because of this, God's Presence left David. David was miserable and longed for God's Presence.

I can imagine David saying, "I've been through too much, gone through too many hard places, too many dry places, gotten overlooked too many times, been hunted down like a criminal too many times, been lied on too many times, been almost devoured and destroyed by my enemies who were in hot pursuit, but God was always with me and He always delivered me.

For a moment I forgot about the goodness of the Lord and I let my flesh, my carnal appetite pull me away from worshipping my God, from giving Him my whole being. But as I look back, I remember how bad it was when I didn't have the ark of the covenant with us; I remember how it felt not to have the Presence of God with us; I remember how it felt to be in a desert place without God's manifested Presence. I remember what I went through to get the Ark from Obededom's house, how discouragement set in when my good intentions went haywire. I remember how when I finally got the Ark back, I danced, I praised God, I sang songs of adoration, I exalted Him.

*AND HIS PRESENCE WAS WITH ME!"*

I can picture David saying "I don't ever want to be without the presence of God again. I don't want my flesh acting up again and getting me out of the will of God." So David cried out in Psalm 51, Lord. I repent - have mercy on me – blot out my transgressions and RENEW my mind so that I won't cave in to the pressures of life. David models for us a man willing to humble himself and repent when he realized that he had let his wilderness experience expel him from God's Presence.

Elijah and Job were two other Old Testament characters who were chosen of God and who faced seasons of wilderness experiences. I will talk about Elijah a little more in another chapter. But let me say here that both of these men suffered from depression, anxiety, fear and low self-esteem during their experiences. But they came out of their wilderness *better*, not bitter. Although their struggles were intense, they did not lose their minds. And neither will you! You can make it through this season and come out stronger, better, wiser and blessed beyond measure.

Yes, there's a down season that goes with being called, chosen and anointed! It's called warfare or the Wilderness Experience where you are under intense pressure and it's designed by the enemy to wear you down, steal your strength and joy and ultimately to destroy your faith and confidence in God, to destroy your "high mountain" testimony, even to destroy your life. But when you hold onto your faith, your declarations, there will always be a ***"BUT GOD" MOMENT where God shows up…!***

Job fell down to the ground under the pressure of his wilderness, **BUT** he used that position to Worship God. He didn't use his mouth to sin like the devil thought he would and wife thought he should BUT instead he released words of affirmation, self-encouragement like David did and worshipped God. *After* he worshipped and *after* he prayed for his friends who mishandled him, he then received the blessing of increase. Double.

Understand, child of God, that *before* every chosen and anointed person gets elevation, before double comes, **pressure comes**. Pressure that the enemy thinks will destroy you when you get tested - in your marriage, finances, friendships, family, physical body, ministry, singleness, spirituality, your business pursuits, your movement.

Let me close this chapter by saying, "You will inevitably have to go through a  wilderness from time to time and your desert places will make you want to murmur and complain like the Israelites. They will make you want to say,    "Lord, I don't like the way You're handling the crisis I'm in. Lord, You're taking too long. Lord, I'm going to die in this storm. Lord, You should have left me in bondage. You should have left me in sin. You should have left me in poverty. At least there I had what I needed."

But children of the Most High God, don't say them. Don't complain when adversities arise. *Close your mouth.* Why? It is because God hears our murmurs and complaints, and as He told Israel in Numbers 14:28-29, "As truly as I live, saith the Lord, as ye have spoken in mine ears, so will I do to you: your carcasses shall fall in this wilderness." They asked for death repeatedly in their complaints and they received what they asked for.

*TRANSFORM THE WORDS OUT OF YOUR MOUTH.*

For those undergoing wilderness pressures, I know that it's rough, but choose to praise God in spite of the situation. Be a ***Wilderness Worshipper***! Check out those biblical trailblazers and people you personally know who have been under pressure but who stayed the course and endured the hardships because they knew God was with them and that they, therefore, could make it through the pressure points.

They are clouds of witnesses who testify:
*"I know somehow, I know some way,*
*we're going to make it.*
*No matter what the test, whatever comes our way,*
*we're going to make it.*

*With Jesus on our side, things will work out fine.*

**We're gonna make it.**

(Wright, Timothy. Performed by Myrna Summers, 1988).

**With God on your side, you can make it!**

# 6

## ~ PREPARATION FOR THE ASSIGNMENT BY THE BROOK CHERITH ~

Elijah the prophet, called and chosen by God, had to find this out for himself, too, that he could make it through the dark times. God sent him out on assignment to prophesy to King Ahab of Israel that the continuous sins of his generation and the previous generations had exhausted God's mercy for them and that judgment was being pronounced upon him. King Ahab was not thrilled when Elijah prophesied that the land would receive no rain, not even dew, for three years. In fact, King Ahab was angry because he knew that their livestock, the people, the grass, the food supply could not survive nor prosper without rain. But God did not allow Elijah to stay in the same vicinity of this angry king but sent him to a place where he could be both protected and instructed.

> "Get thee hence, and turn thee eastward, and hide thyself by the brook Cherith, that is before Jordan" (1 Kings 17:3).

God commanded Elijah to get by himself, not with his servant nor any other prophet, nor any friends, but rather, get off to "yourself, ALONE." God needed Elijah to have a season of isolation where it would be just God and him in communion. It's still that way. Sometimes God needs you to have a season of isolation where it's just you and Him. Why is this season necessary? It is because God is about to pour into you and mold you to prepare you for your NEXT assignment. See, Elijah's next major ministry assignment was coming and God wanted to prepare him so that he could be ready for it. Your next level of ministry is coming, too, but when you aren't ready for it yet, God has to take you through a season of preparation. Your next level of business is coming, but you may not be fully ready for it yet. Your next promotion is coming. Your next level of leadership is coming. Your next level or dimension of ministry is coming. Your next level of wealth is coming, but when you're not quite ready for it yet, God will often tell you to go hide yourself by the brook Cherith (I Kings 17:3). Get away from the crowd. Go on this journey alone, with just Me.

There are several reasons why you must go to this specific brook called Cherith. Cherith means "the cutting place." God sends you to this cutting place so that He can cut out weaknesses in you and refine, mature and develop you. For example, He sends you to Cherith to cut out the spirit of revenge and bring you to a level of development where you can take hateful and lying comments, ridicule, betrayals, etc. without resorting to retaliation.

God knows that He has to get you to a place of *revelation* where you and He can commune and fellowship; where He can talk to you one-on-one; where He can reveal some things about Himself that you don't know, but that you will need to know in this next assignment. And everything He teaches you, He will want you to use it to bless the Kingdom.

God also has to get you to a place of *unreserved thanksgiving* that no matter what you're going through, no matter what you may have lost, no matter how lonely you get, no matter if you're going through a season of lack or a season of *not enough or just barely enough*, that you will be so confident in Him and His provisions that you will yet praise Him.

God showed Elijah that even though I have sent you to this place of isolation and even though you are THERE in the midst of a drought, *I will provide and I will sustain you!* I'm going to let you naturally drink and spiritually drink. Although you're in the midst of a famine, I will bless you to naturally eat and spiritually eat. Men and women of God, the same Word is sent to us today. In the season of a drought, God will bless us to drink of the living water which is the Holy Spirit of God. He will also perform a MIRACLE as He did with Elijah, sending ravens to bring him bread and meat. Elijah was fed from the most unlikely sources, from scavengers that ate dead things. But these particular ravens brought him fresh bread and meat daily. And God sends us His daily fresh BREAD which is the WORD OF LIFE that proceeds out of His mouth to sustain us.

God did this also with another prophet, Moses, while he was undergoing his "Cherith experience." He took him and fed him and personally poured into him His Word, His thoughts, and His ways while Moses was on *the backside of the desert.* Moses had to go by his "Cherith" to have cut out of him carnal things that would deter him from being a great deliverer of God's people out of Egyptian bondage.

Paul, the Apostle, also had a "Cherith" experience out in the Arabian Desert. Because Paul held to an erroneous theology, he went from city to city severely persecuting the Christian Jews. But God wanted to use Paul, but He couldn't use Paul as he was. Paul spent three years in isolation with God who used that time to cut some flaws out of Paul and then set him up to be ready to receive sound teachings and great revelations that he would be destined to deliver to both Jews and especially to the Gentiles.

See, God has a plan for all of our lives. But there are certain things that must be cut away and certain thing that must be learned. One of the first things God wants you to discard at the Cherith Brook is a disobedient spirit and appropriate instead *instant obedience* when He speaks. If you notice, when God told Elijah in I Kings 17:4-5 to leave and journey to the brook, there was not a word of backtalk, not a word of questioning.

> "And it shall be, that thou shalt drink of the brook; and I have commanded the ravens to feed thee there. *So he went and did according unto the word of the LORD*: for he went and dwelt by the brook Cherith, that is before Jordan."

Elijah could move out on God's word like that because he trusted God. He trusted that "God had his back" and would allow only things to happen to him that would serve to work for his good. He learned that when you're down to your very last and then even when that is gone, that God will honor His word to you and provide for your every need. As you can imagine, it is important to *recognize* the voice of God and obey when He speaks.

A second thing God wants you to discard at the brook is complaining and murmuring and to offer instead *praise and thanksgiving*. When things don't go the way that you've planned or the way that you think God should handle situations, be careful that you don't start a cacophony of complaints. Elijah did not complain when the Lord said I have sent those nasty, dead-eating ravens to feed you for awhile. To be transparent, how many of us would have gone merrily on our way singing, "Lord, I Just Want To Thank You!" I doubt many of us would have been grateful for the ravens, but that goes back to show us how important it is for us to **KNOW** the voice of God. If we know that it is God, then we know He's got everything already worked out. Remind yourself that it won't be this way forever. Things will get better.

Third, understand that although I said that it won't last forever, know that it will last for a season. Nobody knows the length of your season at the Cherith brook, but understand that it will be a season of "lockdown" like we had during the coronavirus 2020 pandemic lockdown. A season of staying put, without the company of outside friends and relatives. You **can't hasten nor shorten your spiritual lockdown time.** Elijah couldn't shorten the 3-year lockdown time in Israel because God had set the time duration. So Elijah allowed God to *use the time to profit him.*

Many people did not understand why we had to have a lockdown, but it was working to our advantage, to profit us. It was working for our protection so that our bodies would not be compromised by the virus and we become deathly ill. It was keeping us from other people who may have had the disease and could thereby spread it to us and many others. It was a lonely time, a painful time being away from loved ones, but it was also a necessary time. So many times we don't understand God's ways nor why we have to go down a certain path. Elijah did not complain, but he certainly may have wondered why God had chosen this route for him. Why this season of isolation? Why this season by the "cutting place?"

Looking back in hindsight, Elijah could declare that that season was to prepare him for his NEXT. For his next big battle. For his next major assignment. It was getting him stronger for his encounter with the 850 prophets of Baal and Asherah. It was getting him ready to be *God's fearless mouthpiece to call down fire* from heaven and demonstrate to the idolatrous nation that God alone is God. It was pouring into him the strategies that he would need.

And you too, servant of God, are being prepared for the Great Assignment that is ahead of you. God chose you and anointed you. Somebody reading this knows you're called to deliver people out of various bondages. Somebody's called to heal the sick and infirmed. Somebody's called to open your business that's also going to bless the Kingdom of God. Somebody's called to venture into global ministry. Somebody's called to minister hope and love to the next generation. Somebody's called to get a recording contract and the words you've written and sung are going to break chains...

But God first has to take you through your "Cherith experience" to cut away your flaws, things that could hinder your purpose and assignment. Yes, you are anointed, but you are also a human being, and human beings have character flaws. And that matters to God because character flaws can derail your assignment. Your character really does matter.

Ask King Saul.

He was anointed as King - but character flaws stopped him from becoming all that he could be. And do you know why that was? It was because he did not want to spend time by "the Cherith Brook" and let God reveal and strip him of those flaws. He was a good man but an impatient and fearful one. He revealed this in 1 Samuel 13:8-14 when he demonstrated no patience to wait on Samuel, the prophet and priest whose position qualified him to be the only one authorized to offer the sacrifice to God. King Saul took it upon himself to offer the sacrifice.

When questioned by Samuel as to why he usurped authority, he stated that it was because he had waited seven days for Samuel as he had been told to do, but when Samuel did not readily come, King Saul's soldiers started to desert him. Aware that the Philistines were preparing to attack them and with his army dwindling in size, he decided to take matters into his own hands. Fear and impatience propelled him to step outside of the will of God. They caused him to overstep his boundaries as king and get out of the lane that God had assigned him. Because he recklessly allowed his flesh to drive his actions, his kingdom was taken from him and his seed. King Saul would have profited by using that 7-day lockdown period while he was waiting on Samuel to seek the Lord for guidance and for unwavering faith and to pray and ask God to help him learn patience and obedience. Oh, if only King Saul had taken time to "have a little talk with The Lord," the course of his life could have been so different.

God wanted to talk with King Saul and He also wants to talk to us, too. Sometimes though we're too busy to hear God and sometimes we procrastinate on taking the time to hear God, but when Lockdown comes, when a season of isolation comes, when a season of frustration comes, when a season of despair comes, God gets our attention.

And He tells us, *GO HIDE YOURSELF BY THE CUTTING PLACE.* I need to cut out that jealous spirit, that complaining spirit, that lustful spirit, that self-righteous spirit, that fearful spirit, that low self-esteem spirit, that procrastinating spirit, that doubting spirit…all of the things that want to deter you from fulfilling My will.

It's imperative that you use the time at the "brook" to *hide* yourself in three places. First, **hide yourself in GOD'S WORD**. Study the Word. God is trying to reveal Himself to you in various dimensions. He is trying to cut away arrogance that says I "KNOW" God. You will never know everything about God. His ways are not your ways, and His thoughts are not your thoughts. His ways and thoughts are so much higher than man's. (Isaiah 55:8-9)

But you can find yourself becoming more like The Lord if you humble yourself and say, "Feed me Lord, feed me. Feed me until I think like you, until I walk like you, until I act like you, until I operate in the Spirit like you, until I love like you, until I am merciful like you, until I have compassion like you, until I am patient like you, until I operate in boldness and wisdom like you, until my character is like yours. Feed me, O Lord, feed me Your Word."

Second, *hide yourself in PRAYER*. Call on The Lord like you used to call on Him. Like the old saints used to do. No more popcorn prayer! Set a time and pray the Word! Pray until you start changing from the inside out. Pray until you feel the strength of God returning to you. Pray until you feel empowered to fulfill your assignment. Pray until you get instructions from The Lord. Pray until the atmosphere surrounding you changes. Call on Jesus — JESUS, JESUS! Wail! Travail! Moan! Groan! Hidden thus in prayer, you cannot be found to be defeated by your enemy because The Lord shields you.

Third, *hide yourself in* **WORSHIP**. Sometimes it feels hard to worship God while you're being cut, but remember the vow you made to "bless the Lord at all times." Bless Him and declare by faith that everything is working for your good. Bless and exhort His Name just because He is the Lord God Almighty and worthy of your praise. Boast on how good and great He is! Make His name great by testifying about the mighty acts He's already performed in your life! Give Him the glory that is rightfully due Him. And while you're uplifting His name, the reluctant worship that comes from a depressed spirit will begin to change and it will become fervent and passionate as you pour out your love for God. With a softened and receptive heart, now God can talk more to you of His plans for your life. I speak from experience…

Because don't forget – you were *on lockdown by the brook for a purpose* – to be prepared for your next assignment.

Elijah had a major assignment coming. He had miracles to perform in his future. But he wouldn't have been ready to perform them if he had not hidden away at the Brook Cherith, at the place of cutting, at the place of prayer, at the place of word, at the place of worship, at the place of intimacy with God where he could hear God's next set of instructions.

Like so many people who have been called and chosen by God, I too, had to encounter a Cherith experience – one that would prepare me for my next assignment. I won't lie; it was a painful experience. Cutting never feels good and my flesh didn't want to go that route, but it was needed in order for me to go to the next level of ministry.

My flesh didn't want to go that way when my husband of almost 30 years wanted a divorce. His position was that he just didn't want to be married anymore. He wanted "freedom." I pleaded. I cried. I knew that he was going through the mid-life crisis, so I thought perhaps soon he would snap out of this state that he was in. But he didn't. I tried to do everything that I knew to do to make him happy but to no avail. He wanted that divorce.

What ensued was the most horrific thing I had ever been through. He was the pastor of our church – a thriving church. The church was blessed and poised to go to a higher dimension in ministry. But the devil was angry at our spiritual progress and so he attacked us with an all out assault. Some of the intercessors had seen an attack coming but did not know the specifics of the attack, but just knew that we were to cover our pastor in prayer. And so we did. But like King Saul, my husband operated out of his own free will which God will not override. So satan continued his attack of the head with the intent of destroying the body. The church was split, some defending his actions while others supported us in prayer.

I continued to attend the same church in hopes that he would change his mind although he had stripped me of every ministry position that I held in the church. I endured mockery, ridicule, embarrassment, the spreading of lies, depression and much pain.

Life had become a bitter pill to swallow. One day during my planning period, I sat and cried in my classroom, sobbing, "I can't take any more Lord." I was drowning in my misery. I emailed three friends, hoping that someone would read my plea that said, "Somebody Pray for me!" I needed them to read between the lines and understand that I had hit rock bottom and that I felt "I can't make it. I can't hold on!" I stared at the computer. No response. Then one of them responded and said, "I'm praying!" In a few minutes I felt the manifestation of her intercession and the power of Isaiah 41:10 course throughout my being, "I will strengthen you; I will help you; I will uphold you with the right hand of my righteousness." And surely God did!

My children were deeply wounded by the pending divorce and the unwarranted actions of their father and of some of the members. Some friends did not know how to deal with my new status of a separated, soon-to-be divorced first lady, so they ignored me and I was left primarily alone. Alone.

My finances were in shambles due to my husband filing bankruptcy; my car was repossessed when my husband, who had given it to me for an anniversary gift, quit making the payments without telling me. Due to the bankruptcy my credit score was shot, so every time that I tried to rent an apartment or house, I was turned down. I was desperate! We were losing our house due to foreclosure for non-payments, of which I was unaware. I had no place to go. The Lord showed compassion and touched the heart of an older woman who, though knowing my credit history, allowed me to rent one of her older, smaller houses. A co-worker started picking me up for work. A little later, another friend was able to help me get an older model car where I made modest payments.

I cried out to the Lord numerous times, "Lord, why? Why are you allowing me to go through all of this pain, suffering, hardships, false accusations, betrayal, embarrassment? Why am I being isolated from so many people? Haven't I served you faithfully? Haven't I worshipped you faithfully? Haven't I tried to show love to others? Lord, I don't understand why I'm under such a heavy attack." I didn't know at that time about the warfare that comes with your new assignment nor about the "place of cutting" that we all must go.

But God used that nearly 3-year time frame to lead me by the brook in order for me to hide myself away from the crowd and learn of Him. I didn't realize at the onset that God was about to elevate me for His glory and give me a new major assignment. And I didn't realize that there were some parts of my character that could not go along with this new assignment.

One of the first things that God revealed to me shocked me. I was depressed one evening and decided to go to the movies to see a comedy. I could use some laughter. When the movie ended, I went to my car and sat there, still depressed. Then God spoke to me clearly, "You have made your husband a god! You have put him before Me." I knew that was the voice of God.

As I looked back over my life, I began to recollect times that I had indeed preferred my husband over my God, even before he started pastoring. I began to cry hot tears that turned into sobs as I cried out in repentance to God. I could not believe that I had so dishonored God by putting someone else before Him. God had revealed one of my character defects – being a people pleaser, rather than a God-pleaser – and I didn't like what I was seeing. So God and I used my "alone" time to work on eliminating that defect. God said, You shall have no other gods before Me (Exodus 20:3). God allowed our divorce so that I could see myself and see that my husband was not to be treated as a god.

God also began to show me other defects like being co-dependent, being fearful, being doubtful of my abilities in ministry, and of having low self-esteem. The character flaws that God knew I couldn't take into my new assignment, He revealed to me and then began the process of stripping me of them. It was a painful cutting season. I didn't even realize some of those flaws were in me.

I stayed before the Lord in prayer. I was already an intercessor, but in this season I became more ardent, more committed, more prayerful, more studious in His Word. The devil wasn't too happy about me becoming more in tune with God so one night around midnight, he sought to take my life. I was lying in bed trying to go to sleep, but I couldn't because the devil's voice got louder and louder in my ear as he spoke repeatedly that he was going to kill me that night. I was afraid to go to sleep. I prayed and rebuked the thoughts, but the thoughts only intensified. I knew I needed prayer reinforcement, so I called my young adult son who immediately and profoundly began to intercede and rebuke the evil spirit. He then began to speak life over me. The enemy left. Peace came over me and I went to sleep.

I knew then that the Lord had a special assignment for me that the devil did not want me to fulfill. He was trying to kill me while I was still at the brook Cherith. It was like the devil thinking that he could take Elijah out while he was in the middle of a drought and famine, but God sustained Elijah and He sustained me. While I hid in the secret place of God, God provided for my every need and worked on developing my character. This was necessary because I would need to be strong to handle the next assignment. It was an awesome "NEXT" coming, but it wouldn't be one for the fearful or for the faint- hearted!

My divorce was final a year later and three months following that, the three-year work done on me at Cherith paid off. Nine years after being called to preach, God elevated me to the pastorate of a new ministry called Recover All Christian Temple. He put the pastoral mantle on me that my late father had worn for years; now the mantle was on me to feed a new flock of sheep. God instilled boldness in me and a determination to let God use me however He saw fit. It's amazing, but I never saw myself as a pastor while growing up. But God saw me, a little shy and timid girl, and He called, chose and anointed me at the Cherith brook to be the vessel that He would use.

As the years passed, God continued to give me assignments. He moved upon my state diocesan and former Presiding Bishop of the PAW, Bishop Charles H Ellis, III, to elevate me to District Elder, an overseer position of several churches at our state conference level of the Pentecostal Assemblies of the World, Inc. Then in 2018, God gave me my next assignment as the first female Vice-Chairperson of our state conference. In 2021 God gave me an online platform to teach "Lunching On The Word," a weekly Facebook Live and Instagram broadcast with viewership reaching those in the United States and in foreign countries. In 2022 The Lord opened another door of ministry with a Zoom platform targeting hurting women dealing with low self-esteem, anxiety and depression with the Whole Woman Care Ministry. Today, I understand my assignment - I have been called to sit in the seat of Deborah, the Old Testament warrior, to lead an army in countering the warfare of the enemy and to help God's people win victories.

None of these assignments could have happened without that Cherith experience. Men and women of God, you have to hear me. Young people, you have to hear me. God used that period of Isolation to cut away some of my character flaws, cut away my dependency on others and taught me how to trust Him. He cut away fears and doubts. And He's not finished with me yet. He's still working on me because there is yet work to be done in the Kingdom. And every assignment comes with a little more cutting away of "your flesh."

And I can surmise that God is doing the same with you–cutting away any carnality, any pride, any excuses, any doubts, any fears, etc. But though the devil means the upheavals to work for your evil, God has already determined that it will work for your good. That one scripture, Romans 8:28, held me together during my crisis more than any of the others. I had to trust that "*...all things work together for good to them that love God, to them who are the called according to His purpose.*"

God uses every one of your negative experiences for *your* good! Everybody can't go where God is taking you. Everybody can't endure the same Cherith experience. The older brothers of Joseph couldn't have withstood what Joseph withstood - ALONE - away from family and friends. And they couldn't have made it in later years as the second in command over the Egyptian empire. They hadn't paid the cost of that oil, that anointing. God had a purpose that only Joseph was ordained and suited to fulfill.

Know that God's got a purpose behind your pain, your struggles, your season of isolation, your CHERITH BROOK EXPERIENCE. There are greater things that He's going to accomplish in your life, so keep your ears attuned to the Master.

Chapter

# 7

## ~ CHOSEN, BUT NOW THE BROOK'S DRIED UP~

When the brook dries up, what do you? Remember, this is the place where God has been providing for you in the famine and it's the place where you have gotten closer to Him. But now it seems you're facing another dilemma during this season – a drying up of provisions, of resources; when you see it drying up, day by day, like Elijah did in 1 Kings 17:7, what do you do?

Understand that Elijah had been nourished with natural and spiritual provisions. Naturally, God had sent ravens to feed him by the brook and had led him to the brook to quench his thirst. Spiritually, he and the Lord had communed. Everything was making more sense to Elijah as he stayed in a hidden place and prepared himself for ministry. But then, his water provision dried up. Now the one thing that you can't go a long time without is water. Your body must have water. It can only last "a few days at most without water" (Johnson May 14, 2019) while "in general, it is likely that a person could survive between one and two months without food." (Barrell March 17, 2020)

Here's the test! What do you do? What do you do when it seems that God has stopped providing and it seems like the well has run dry? What would you do? What do most of us do? The answer is, independent of God, we try to figure out our next step.

But let's look at something David did in 1st and 2nd Samuel; David did something remarkable at least **nine** times. Anytime something is repeated in the Bible that means *it's worth noting*. Nine times the Scripture says **"DAVID ENQUIRED OF THE LORD"** for direction and guidance! *NINE TIMES! (1 Samuel 23:1-3, 4-5, 10-11, 12-14; 30:8-9; 2 Samuel 2:1-2; 5:17-21, 22-25; 21:1)*

Now why would David stop and ask God about his next move? It is because you can put no confidence in your flesh, in your thoughts! You should never put yourself in the position of God as if you know *everything*! What does the Word of God say in Proverbs 3:5-6?

> "Trust in the LORD with all your heart, and do not lean on your own understanding. In all your ways acknowledge Him, and He will make your paths straight."

Or will we turn to our own strategies and endure the resulting consequences? (cf. Isa. 50:10-11; Jer. 2:12-13)

David enquired of the Lord those nine times because he knew that he did *not* know what to do. He did *not* know how to handle King Saul who was desperately trying to kill him; he did *not* know how to handle the Philistine enemies nor the Amalekite enemies who were trying to destroy David, his family, his army and his nation.

David asked the Lord for counsel each time, even if it seemed like the attack was set up the same way as a previous one. He did not presume that he knew which angle to strike from, which path to avoid, which direction to pursue. Leaning on his own understanding of which strategy to use would have caused his death and all those who were with him. Enquiring of the Lord, listening to His answers and obeying His voice saved their lives.

It behooves us to seek counsel from God each and every time we are faced with a "dried up brook," to ask Him to order our steps to where our NEXT should take us. We cannot afford to feel that we don't need God's guidance because we assume that we are so "tight with God like that," that we are such committed workers in the church, that we give cheerfully to the poor – in other words that our works please God so much and that we are on such good speaking terms with the Lord, that we forget to do a most important thing – and that is, *to listen to the voice of God for instructions.*

Let's look at how Elijah the prophet met his test. He's a role model for us today as was King David when presented with a challenge. ***Before*** the challenge came, *before* the test came, Elijah was *maintaining a lifestyle* of prayer, worship and intimacy with God – even there at the Cutting Place of Cherith. This lifestyle kept him in tune with God. His worship bonded him with God. His prayer life was a two-way conversation with God, where he both talked and listened. I can imagine his prayer time including a request to the Lord where he would say, "Lord, **ANOINT MY EAR GATES** so that I can hear you clearly, with clarity."

In order to live, to make it through the difficult days ahead of him, Elijah had to do three things that we, too, must do. He had to listen, he had to wait for specific instructions and lastly, he had to obey the instructions. Immediately after  the famine was first prophesied by Elijah in I Kings 17:1, God spoke to him in verse 3, "Get thee hence…" Get away from King Ahab. Ahab will try to kill you. So Elijah knew he must leave and leave quickly, but where was he to go? By *continuing* to listen to God, he got specific instructions, "…turn thee eastward, and hide thyself by the brook Cherith, that is before Jordan."  He waited on God for the crucial additional information that would need to be given – how he would survive in this famine. God, in His omniscience, had already prepared the provisions and told him, "And it shall be, that thou shalt drink of the brook: and I have commanded the ravens to feed thee there." (I Kings 17:4)

After hearing the instructions from the Lord, the Bible says in verse 5, "So he went and did according unto the word of the Lord." His obedience brought him the blessing of provisions. But after awhile, "the brook dried up, because there had been no rain in the land" (verse 7). But Elijah, who trusted God in the first part of his test, knew how to lean and depend on The Lord, how to wait patiently for Him to speak. He knew God's eyes were upon him and that God already had foreseen the brook drying up, had already foreseen the complications in the "forecast" and had already made a way of escape. Because he knew God was not through using him for His business, he *waited* on God to speak. "And the word of the Lord came unto him saying…"

Elijah used the same pattern that worked before. He listened, waited for specific instructions, waited for additional information and then obeyed. Faith cometh by hearing the word of the Lord. Elijah heard, ARISE. Then the *specific* instructions came in verse 9: "…get thee to Zarephath, which belongeth to Zidon, and dwell there:" Additional information was given and Elijah heard of the most unlikely source of his new provisions: "behold, I have commanded a widow woman there to sustain thee."

God works in mysterious ways, His wonders to behold.

"So [in faith] he arose and went to Zarephath." The practice of listening to God and obeying God in a most stressful time of his life caused Elijah "to live throughout the three-year famine and not die." It was important that Elijah live! *His purpose required that he live.* There were yet miracles for him to perform and his most major assignment to fulfill.

What do you do when your brook dries up? When you have to leave the comfort of knowing every day exactly what you will have to sustain you? What do you do when your life, your future is at stake? When saving your marriage is at stake? Do you figure out a plan to do this or to do that? What do you do when saving your ministry, your career, your relationship with others is at stake; or when promotions, business plans, business, education, or financial futures are at stake? What do you do? I'll tell you.

You follow Elijah's lead and you LISTEN, LISTEN, LISTEN TO GOD. You walk by faith and not by sight, and you obey God.

**WHY DO WE NEED THIS GUIDANCE?** It is because *we have never been this way before and we don't know how to navigate it.* Elijah had never faced such a famine – a famine that he had prophesied into existence, by the way, but regardless of that, he needed divine guidance to get through it.

Similarly, in the 21$^{st}$ century, we had never faced a PANDEMIC before; in fact, in our lifetime, most of us had never heard the word used before. Most of us had never faced, even more recently, a tripledemic (threesome disease occurring simultaneously): covid, rsv and the flu.

And neither had some of you ever faced a divorce before, nor neglect and abandonment, nor betrayals, nor abuses, nor lawsuits, nor harassment, nor loss of jobs, nor the death of a loved on, nor ministry pitfalls...

So what one thing did the pandemic reveal, which is also what our struggles today reveal? It is *OUR NEED OF GOD,* His wisdom and His strategies.

Lord, give us the grace to wait on you for instructions, then for further specific instructions and finally, for the additional information that will help enlighten, preserve and motivate us while we go through the difficult days.

Consider this: if Elijah had chosen his own path, if he had gone the way he thought best instead of getting directions from the Lord, he could have perished in the famine – without having fulfilled the assignments of The Lord.

*Chapter*

# 8

## ~ YOU CAN'T DIE-YOU'RE
## TO VALUABLE ~

The devil can throw so much at you until it can make you *feel like* listening to your own voice, following your own plan and ultimately quitting and forgetting all about your assignment. But this is no time to "throw in the towel" or quit or yield to your fleshly yearning for death because of the heartaches, sufferings, traumas you are enduring. No one denies that your suffering is intense, but I implore you, don't die; don't refuse to press forward. There's a world out there, full of people, that are waiting on YOU to hang on in there and fulfill the purpose for which you were born. And *you were born on purpose* to be used by God to bring salvation, healings and deliverance to people. It is the same purpose for which Jesus came to this earth. He speaks of being anointed for this assignment in Luke 4:18-19 and has commissioned us with the same assignment:

> *"The Spirit of the Lord is upon me, because he hath anointed me to preach the gospel to the poor; he*

*hath sent me to heal the brokenhearted, to preach
deliverance to the captives, and recovering of sight
to the blind, to set at liberty them that are bruised,
To preach the acceptable year of the Lord."*

Even the Old Testament believers were commissioned
with this assignment. Some fulfilled it in the political arena,
the marketplace, the palace, the evangelistic field, the
battleground, in the community, in places of worship, etc.
Most of them did so while under scrutiny and intense
pressures where they could have denied the call on their
lives and surrendered their will to live.

*But Joseph didn't. Moses didn't. Johua didn't. David
didn't. Deborah didn't. Esther didn't. Daniel didn't. Elijah
didn't. Jeremiah didn't. And in the New Testament, Peter
didn't. Stephen didn't. Paul didn't. Timothy didn't. Mary
Magdalene didn't. Joanna didn't. Junia didn't and a host of
other witnesses didn't.*

They didn't because they knew that they had within
them the power and the authority to rescue countless people
who had a need to be delivered out of the hand of the
enemy.

Joseph's assignment was to deliver Israel and
surrounding nations from death. But on the way to fulfilling

his assignment, he encountered much physical and emotional pain. The kind of pain that could make a person truly give up. But Joseph had been given a dream as a teenager that he could not shake, that spoke of him one day being in a position of power; that position would not be for Joseph to gain glory, but God had already ordained that in that prominent position he would save much people alive.

Joseph was unaware that his journey to prominence would include being thrown by his jealous brothers into a pit that could have killed him; or being ripped from his family and sold into Egyptian slavery; or being sexually harrassed by his boss's wife; certainly not of being thrown into jail when he wouldn't comply with the sexual advances; nor of being left in prison for about 13 years for a crime that he didn't commit; all of this and more he endured so that he could be in position to fulfill his major assignment. He went through all of that to have a "prison platform" with the Pharoah who had had a dream that only Joseph could interpret, that only Joseph had the solution for. Because of Joseph recognizing God's providential hand in the upheavals of his life, he was ready to pardon his brothers when they came to Egypt looking for food during the seven-year famine. He blessed them and said, don't be afraid that I am going to get revenge on you for all that you did against me. Rather, he spoke in Genesis 50:20,

> "...*ye thought evil against me;* but *God meant it unto good, to bring to pass, as it is this day,* **to save much people alive.**"

In other words, Joseph was on assignment. And he elected to live and not let the pressures of life overthrow or cancel his assignment of being a deliverer and a strategist, saving many people. If he had chosen to wallow in self-pity or drown his sorrows or just plain give up on life, then the Messiah would not have come down through the lineage of Judah because Judah, Joseph's brother, would have been swallowed up by the famine and destroyed. Can you imagine this: *One man's obedience to his assignment brought to us the Savior, Jesus Christ,* who in turn, fulfilled His assignment of dying on the cross to redeem us from our sins and to give us eternal life. If Joseph had backed out of his assignment, then where would any of us be today? All of these Old and New Testament believers walked in their calling, regardless of the cost.

Moses was called to be a deliverer, to bring God's people out of harsh Egyptian servitude into their own land of freedom and prosperity. While that may seem to be an easy task, it was not because Moses had to deal with a stubborn, rebellious, idolatrous, complaining people who *turned an 11-day trek into a 40-year arduous journey.* When the people's ways became intolerable, Moses almost quit and even asked God to take his life (Numbers 11:15), but Moses had been called by God to that assignment from the burning bush (Exodus 3:7-8). Although Moses's burden was quite heavy, God let him know you're not carrying this assignment alone. I'm carrying you Moses and I'm giving you 70 men to help you with the load. Moses had to retract his death wish and live. He could not die. He could not quit. Why? Because there were millions of people who still needed to see God as a strong Deliverer, who still needed to possess the promise of God. And Moses was the man God qualified to fulfill that assignment and bring them to the border of their Promised Land.

Joshua was then called to be a spritual and military leader and take them all the way into the Promised Land. But possessing the land required Joshua to lead the men into 13 hard battles. Joshua was distraught at times, discouraged at other times, but he proved himself to be an extraordinary leader who led the people triumphantly into conquering the Promised Land, thus fulfilling his assignment.

Many of you know the story of David and the calling on his life to be a king and a prophet. Many times David had to encourage himself in psalms, prayer, and worship to stay the course on his assignment for he was being attacked on so many different levels. But David never gave up his throne nor his assignment. It was the fulfilling of his assignment that led to the Messiah coming through his lineage to be King forever.

Deborah also fulfilled her assignment in several ways – she was a prophetess, the first female judge to govern both spiritual and political affairs in Israel. She was a courageous, mighty warrior and military strategist who didn't let her gender prevent her from leading the Israeli army into battle when the general was too afraid to go. Fear could have stopped her from engaging in her purpose – fear of peers, fear of the enemy, fear of naysayers, fear of death, but if she had given into that, she would have caused the annihilation of her people. She recognized that this assignment of a warrior on the battlefield is mine – I must fulfill it.

If she had not been also on her post as a fair and impartial judge, many people would not have benefited from her sound wisdom thereby much chaos and strife among individuals, families and neighbors could have erupted in her city. She recognized that this assignment, too, is mine – I must fulfill it.

There are so many others that we could talk about who did not forget why they were put on this earth. Knowing their purpose, they fulfilled their assignment. Queen Esther fulfilled her assignment as the deliverer of her people who were about to be slaughtered by Haman (Read the book of Esther).

Daniel fulfilled his as a prophet and high-ranking government official who prayed relentlessly and received revelations and prophesied even when it almost cost his life in the lions' den. (Read the book of Daniel).

Jeremiah, the weeping prophet, fulfilled his prophetic assignment although the people turned a deaf ear to him. He recognized, "It's my assignment whether they hear or not, whether they hate me enough to throw me in a pit and in prison." (Read the book of Jeremiah).

And in the New Testament, Peter didn't shrink away from fulfilling his assignment as an apostle, teacher, healer and as the one who opened the door to salvation by giving the key message of the gospel in Acts 2. Peter's preaching of that message on the day of Pentecost convicted the hearts of 3,000 people who received the message, were baptized, filled with the Holy Ghost and added to the

Church. Because of Peter's fulfilling his assignment, people from that time to now have access to the kingdom of heaven.

Mary Magdalene fulfilled hers as one who walked closely with Jesus as His disciple and as the first proclaimer of the astounding truth that Jesus Christ had arisen from the dead. Her eyewitness account instilled faith in many believers and reignited hope back into those who were downcast because of Jesus's crucifixion. She, Joanna and several other women were also key financial supporters of Jesus' ministry and the further spreading of the gospel.

The Samaritan woman at the well could have kept quiet her encounter with Jesus and if she had, a whole village would have never received the good news that Jesus had come to save everyone, not just the Jewish people (St. John 4). But she had a pressing assignment to inform the villagers that the Messiah that they had been waiting for had come and that He was there to give them eternal life.

Junia served her calling as a female apostle in the Bible (Romans 16:7). She was not one of the original 12 apostles, but Paul declared her to be a prominent apostle who joined the ranks of other apostles such as Barnabas, Silas, Timothy, Adronicus, Epaphroditus and Matthias; as an apostle she was sent out to plant churches, to proclaim the message of God, to equip the church's initial leaders and the body of believers for the work of the ministry. She did not let gender prejudices stop her from fulfilling her mission, for in the body of Christ and in the ministry work of the Kingdom, "there is neither Jew or Greek, there is neither bond nor free, there is neither male nor female: for ye are all one in Christ Jesus" (Galatians 3:28). She was persecuted and suffered for the cause of Christ along with Paul, her co-labourer in the Gospel. (Preato, Daniel. "Junia, a Female Apostle." April 26, 2019)

And certainly, it is well-noted and documented that Paul didn't shrink from his assignment although he faced many dangers. His gratitude to God for forgiving him of his sins and his atrocities and persecutions against the Church before becoming a believer propelled him to yield to the call on his life as an apostle.

Although Paul endured much persecution, he determined to rise above all of his heartaches and sufferings for he was more concerned about the lives that he had to touch with the powerful message of the good news of salvation and deliverance than he was about sitting passively by while people died without the knowledge of the birth, death and resurrection of Jesus Christ. He had been called by God, chosen by Him to fulfill this mission.

The rewards of Paul's labor produced much fruit. Paul is highly regarded as one of the two or three most influential persons in the New Testament who, in fulfilling his assignment, ministered to more Gentiles than any other of the apostles which caused Christianity to spread beyond Jewish borders. His ministry fulfilled The Lord's commission that we "Go ye into all the world, and preach the gospel to every creature" (Mark 16:15).

Can you imagine your spiritual life and development without the ministry work of Paul? It's hard to imagine, isn't it? Likewise, there are many today who need your ministry, in whatever capacity it may be, in order for them to holistically heal, develop, mature and further the cause of Christ.

No, you cannot die nor give up. There is just too much ministry in you that must be poured out on others. Too many lives are at stake. You cannot stifle or quench the Spirit of God in you and go sit down on the pew of "do nothing." You must do as these biblical heroes did - LIVE AND FULFILL YOUR ASSIGNMENTS. Remember they were not superheroes; they were mere mortals who loved The Lord. You must be a Queen Esther and fight your fear, as she did, and fulfill your assignment so that your nation might live. You must live and be an Elijah so that you can develop believers in the School of Prophets to carry on the work of The Lord. And you must live, Elijah, to pass your mantle onto Elisha, the next generation. You must heed the directive given to Paul: *you can not die* in that shipwreck nor die from the stoning or floggings nor can you die from the venomous snake bite – *__you must live__* to get to Rome to fulfill your assignment to witness the gospel before the Emperor Caesar.

Understand that there are too many men waiting, too many women, too many children and youth crying out internally for salvation and deliverance. They are in need of your gift, of your calling. Silver and gold you may not have to give, but such gifting, such ministry as you have, give unto them (Acts 3:6). They are on your jobs, in your schools and colleges, in your communities, on your street, in your families, on the sports field, on social media, in your churches, in the government and in the military. They are everywhere that you are.

No one else can quite handle this assignment like you can – God has equipped you in a very unique way. Now, go and get ready to use your gifts, skills, creativity, intercession, administration skills, leadership skills, speaking skills, etc. that people may live and come to know this Jesus Christ that you love.

# Chapter

# 9

## ~ ASSIGNMENT –
## ATMOSPHERE CHANGERS~

Your next assignment is a major one. It is to shift the atmosphere in your environment. The atmosphere in the world today is an ungodly, idolatrous one. It's filled with pain, hurt, trauma, selfishness, greed, unforgiveness, bitterness, hatred, narcissism, betrayals, violence, anger and other emotions and behaviors triggered by the devil.

Such was the case during the reign of King Ahab and Queen Jezebel. The Bible says in I Kings 16:30 that King Ahab did more evil than any of the predecessors (kings) before him. I Kings 21:25 shows the complicity of his wife to urge him on to do more and more evil and to cause the people of Israel to set up idol gods and worship them. The atmosphere was no longer like the one of King David's time where he and the people worshipped God wholeheartedly (I Kings 8:62; 2 Samuel 6:12-19). The people had now turned from serving God and were worshipping the idol god, Baal.

God sent Elijah on a major national assignment to turn the hearts of the people back to Him. To do that Elijah challenged the 450 prophets of Baal to a demonstration of power by their god versus the demonstration of power by The Lord Jehovah.

> *"Let them therefore give us two bullocks; and let them choose one bullock for themselves, and cut it in pieces, and lay it on wood, and put no fire under: and I will dress the other bullock, and lay it on wood, and put no fire under: And call ye on the name of your gods, and I will call on the name of the Lord: and the God that answereth by fire, let him be God. And all the people answered and said, It is well spoken."* (I Kings 18:23-24)

Although they called on Baal from morning to evening, their god did not answer. He did not listen to their anguished cries that he consume the sacrifice and thus prove that he was a prayer answering god and that he was therefore the one worthy of worship. (Read the full story in I Kings 18:17-39).

It was then Elijah's turn to call on His God. This was the great moment that God had been waiting on – for Elijah to fulfill this crucial assignment in the demonstration of

God's power that would change the spiritual climate in Israel; that would change the idolatrous atmosphere to a God atmosphere; that would change the Baal-chasers to God-chasers; that would rid the land of the 450 false prophets of Baal; and that would raise the worship level to God and to God alone.

When Elijah rebuilt the altar, He called out to God with whom he had a good relationship:

*"Lord God of Abraham, Isaac, and of Israel, let it be known this day that thou art God in Israel, and that I am thy servant, and that I have done all these things at thy word. Hear me, O Lord, hear me, that this people may know that thou art the Lord God, and that thou hast turned their heart back again. Then the <u>fire of the Lord fell</u>, and consumed the burnt sacrifice, and the wood, and the stones, and the dust, and licked up the water that was in the trenches." (I Kings 18:36-38)*

God answered <u>Immediately</u> **BY FIRE.** *IN THAT MOMENT THE SPIRITUAL CLIMATE CHANGED FROM COLD TO HOT!*

**39** And when all the people saw it, they fell on their faces: and they said, The Lord, he is the God; the Lord, he is the God.

**They declared unequivocally that "The Lord, he is the God; the Lord, he is the God."**

The people's worship and proclamation showed that *Elijah's preparations for this assignment had not been in vain.* Going into isolation at the brook, spending time with God and listening to His directions, following His guidance, allowing the Lord to "cut" away his flaws at Cherith and building him up to the point where his faith was strong had all paid off.

ELIJAH WAS ON ASSIGNMENT TO MAKE A MAJOR IMPACT.

And he did because *he was prepared!*

And for some of you, your next assignment is to <u>change the spiritual climate</u> in your families, in your community, in your schools, in the generations who have not heard of God, in marriages, your workplace, in the government, in the entertainment system, in your churches and in our nation and in every place and institution where God is not honored and worshipped.

God is indeed preparing you for your next assignment. It might be a local assignment, a community assignment, a corporation assignment, a regional assignment, a national assignment or a global assignment.

Why are you needed? You are needed because many today have turned from God and are serving all types of idols that have become more important to them than God. They are worshipping wealth, power, self, entertainment, sex, Eastern religions, materialism, spouses and children, technology, social media influencers and a host of others. But God's command still holds true today as it did in Exodus 20:3 when He spoke, "You shall have no other gods before Me."

I reiterate and stress the importance of your calling. God is preparing you for your next assignment - TO CHANGE THE SPIRITUAL CLIMATE IN YOUR SPHERE OF INFLUENCE and to show forth His light and love to those who have been seduced and deceived by the devil's tactics.

You are on assignment to tear down strongholds; to speak resurrection to dead stuff; to speak sound doctrine; to encourage and strengthen the brethren; to give sound and

Godly wisdom; to write that uplifting book of poetry or book of fiction or inspirational nonfiction; to educate and empower with the Word of God; to heal the sick and infirmed; to be an entrepreneur to help finance Kingdom work; to rescue the young people from the streets; to save our men; to enhance our school system; to write the lyrics to your story of struggles and pain that turned and worked for your good; to be the social media engineer who can get your pastor's messages around the globe; to be among the creative arts people whose dancing is so anointed that chains of depression are broken off them.

You are on assignment to reach out to abused women, men or children and bring healing and beauty for their ashes; to be the visionary or financier of affordable and quality housing for the homeless, for the youth in foster care who have aged out, the elderly and low income families; to be the telephone care outreach person to the shut in, to seniors, to pandemic and long covid patients; to help the special needs population; to spread the gospel anywhere, whenever and however you can; to set captives free; to be the intercessors and prayer warriors…

EVERYONE HAS AN ASSIGNMENT to awaken a dying and indifferent world, to change the spiritual climate, to bring life and restoration, to bring enlightenment where the acknowledgment has to come that THE LORD, <u>HE IS THE TRUE AND ONLY GOD!</u>

To all of the Elijahs out there, GOD IS PREPARING
YOU *<u>N O W</u>*
FOR YOUR N E X T!!!

Chapter

# 10

## ~ FULFILLING THE ASSIGNMENT-
## THIS IS THE DAY! ~

This is the day that the Lord has made – for you – to step out and declare as Mary, the mother of Jesus, did when she spoke to the angel who told her that she would bear a child, although she was a virgin. There would be no natural means of conception, no artificial insemination, but the angel proclaimed that "the Holy Ghost shall come upon thee, and the power of the Highest shall overshadow thee" and cause an immaculate conception. Mary's response was *this* Day, *this* Moment "…**be it unto me according to thy word (Luke 1:35, 38)."**

**May the Holy Ghost awaken what He has put in your spiritual womb. May you nurture that holy thing and birth it because it is destined to add glory to the Kingdom of God.**

I remember God *re*awakening what He put in my womb. Sometimes we let our assignments lie dormant until God gives us that nudge that says, "It's time to be about My business." It was during a time of worship in my prayer time about a year ago when God reminded me emphatically that He had created me with purpose, power and authority for the fulfilling of my assignment. The fact that He still wanted to use me after a season of procrastination filled me with awe and praises. Here's a little of the praise that I wrote down that day to honor and thank the Lord.

> "Thank you Lord for giving me creative ability, creative forces to operate on this earth. To create what has not been before; to birth new things, innovative things that have been put into me! Oh Lord, I am so unworthy, but yet you have chosen me.

> Everything that's in this world is because you Lord God created it. You called for it to come into existence. You created everything that is!

> EVERYTHING - the air we breathe, the amoeba, the droplets of water, rain clouds, sunshine to create a path of vision in the early dawn of darkness AND to overturn night; sunshine to warm our bodies, to create the photosynthesis plant process that feeds us.

You created us in Your own image. You created us to be creative, innovative and to create just like you. YOU created us to act and dominate just like you, with power and authority. YOU created us to speak the word that ignites change. And whatever is not in you Lord Jesus, it should therefore not be in me! For I am made in your image and in your likeness. And I thank and honor You Lord for that.

I THANK YOU THAT I WAS NOT CREATED TO BE BOUND NOR TO BE IN BONDAGE TO ANYTHING!!! I am a representation of you. I represent You. And in that calling, I must walk, I must operate. I must synthesize in my spirit who I am in the Lord and I must pass this message onto others." Amen.

Release what is in you and do not let fear hold you back. Let me reiterate a few things about Christ, your model, example, mentor.

WHAT CHRIST HAS NEVER BEEN…

Pastor John Hannah of Chicago says repeatedly in his messages that "Christ was not AND is not a punk!" He is not fearful, nor cowardly. Christ told satan, "get behind me" Matt. 4:1-11. That means to physically position oneself (or be positioned) behind someone or something. In other words, to GO AWAY.

Christ told the ferocious storm to be still though it was raging around Him too. Now, the disciples had no reason to be afraid. They were going to a place where Jesus wanted to go to do ministry. And since God-in-the-flesh was right there with them in the boat, there was nothing that would keep them from getting there. Yet they panicked. Scripture tells us

> "Then He arose and rebuked the wind, and said to the sea, "Peace, be still!" And the wind ceased and there was a great calm. And he said unto them, Why are ye so fearful? How is it that ye have no faith? And they feared exceedingly, and said one to another, What manner of man is this, that even the wind and the sea obey him?" (Mark 4:39-41).

They were terrified, but Christ was not. He knew power and authority were invested in Him. Therefore, he had no reason to be mealy-mouthed around the enemy who was trying to stop his destiny so that He could not fulfill His assignment.

We're called to be *Just Like Jesus*!! Not punks! Not

fearful, but exercising EXOUSIA AND DUNAMIS
POWER AND AUTHORITY as we fulfill our assignments,
using the Power of God to calm storms meant to destroy us
in our cities, families, in our homes, churches, workplace,
in our health, in our nation and in our world.

Where is the power and authority of Jesus to still the
noise of many turbulent waters today? IT'S IN YOU AND
IT'S IN ME!

We can't be running scared either! After all, Who do we
serve? Who called us? Who chose us? Who chose YOU –
before the world was even created? Who anointed you with
the Holy Ghost power and authority? Luke 10:9 says:
"Behold, I give unto you power to tread on serpents and
scorpions, and over all the power of the enemy: and
nothing shall by any means hurt you."


WHO CHRIST IS ...

strong, bold, the Lion of Judah, courageous, determined,
wise, knowledgeable, compassionate, merciful, loving and
faithful. He is the Anointed One sent to destroy yokes
(Luke 4:18). He gave unselfishly of Himself to bless the
world. THAT SAME SPIRIT OF THE LORD IS UPON
YOU, TOO.

Release what God has put into you. This is your season

to release what He downloaded into you so that you can speak life and deliverance into the people of your community, your family, and anywhere that God sends you. Be a sharp shooter in the spirit. Seek God to know exactly what is wrong and where the laser weapon should be directly pointed.

*RELEASE* what you have… in your mouth…in your hands.

*RELEASE* your voice, your creative words.

*RELEASE* your intercessory prayers.

*RELEASE* your vision to see.

*RELEASE* your ears to hear.

*RELEASE* your anointing.

*RELEASE* deliverance.

*RELEASE* the word of life over the dry bones.

*RELEASE* life and recovery over that which should be alive.

*This is your season* to step out into the field in which God has called you. This is *your* season to use your gifts, talents, skills, creativity, voice and your power and authority to change the spiritual climate in the area that He has chosen you.

This is your day to say "YES" to the Lord and to all of His plans for your life, for

**GOD HAS SPECIFICALLY CHOSEN YOU FOR THIS ASSIGNMENT.**

# Afterword

My assignment to feed you the gospel, to spread it through the publishing of this book, to educate you, inspire you and equip you to reach others WITH THIS WORD so that you can, in turn, EMPOWER THEM is nearly complete.

**Before I end "my" assignment, let me pray with you and encourage you to move Forward into the work in which God has called you.**

Lord Jesus, I praise and honor You for your love and for the privilege You have given each of us to extend Your kingdom on this earth. I pray that each reader will realize that this is his or her season to release the flow of the Holy Ghost, to allow the fresh Wind of the Holy Ghost to hover over his or her gifts, skills, creativity, and prayer life. And Lord, may you rekindle in each person the zeal and the anointing to reach souls and the anointing to do effective ministry for the Kingdom.

Let each person declare who he or she is in the Kingdom— "I'm the chosen of God, I'm the chosen apple of God's eye, I'm the anointed, chosen servant of the Lord, whether I'm on the mountain top or in the valley. I'm the chosen, called out one spurred on and sent out by faith to fulfill my assignment. Faith is my vehicle that transports me through my various assignments."

I declare that what you speak, according to the Will and Word of God shall come to pass. There shall be a great performance of what God has spoken over your life, for faith in Christ is your valid and legal authority to execute power over all the power of the enemy (Luke 10:19). And as an obedient servant of God, you will speak and act and the evil forces tormenting the earth shall be subdued. You will demonstrate that you are a CHOSEN VESSEL OF GOD WHO IS FULFILLING YOUR LUKE 4:18 ASSIGNMENT IN THE KINGDOM.

*P.S. Dear Reader, I applaud each of you who embraces your assignment.*

*__This__ assignment given me is now complete - now on to my next one . . .*

# Epilogue

*"And David enquired at the Lord, saying, Shall I pursue after this troop? shall I overtake them? And he answered him, Pursue: for thou shalt surely overtake them, and without fail recover all.*
*~(1 Samuel 30:8)~*

*God had spoken to me during my wilderness experience and told me that he would give me "double for my shame" (Isaiah 61:7). In other words, He would bless me for all that I had endured.*

Three and a half years after my separation and subsequent divorce, my husband, who had resigned from the pastorate of the church, called me out of the blue. He said to me that God had spoken to him in such a distinct way that there was no denying that it was Christ talking, and said to him, "Go home to your wife." My husband responded, "But I'm not married anymore." God said, "Go home to your wife." He knew intuitively what that meant.

He later picked up the phone, called me and initiated reconciliation. He said to me, "I never stopped loving you and I really don't know what got into me to make me do the things that I did. Please forgive me for all the pain I caused…!"

I still loved him, but I was cautious. His mid-life crisis had indeed caused much pain and I wondered if he was fully through it.

It seemed he was and forgiveness and healing ensued and we remarried.

I learned that it is never too late for God to restore broken pieces. I also learned that God is faithful to His Word as is stated in Numbers 23:19. God did restore to me "double" for everything that I had lost. He gave me double for my lost 3 1/2 years of marriage, He repaired my bleak financial situation, gave me a brand new, better home, increased my ministry opportunities and gave me much favor.

My husband worked alongside me at the church that I founded and pastored as the assistant pastor until his untimely death. The church, amazingly, had been aptly named BEFORE our reconciliation - Recover All Christian Temple.

# Bibliography

*Chapter 5*

Wright, Timothy Rev. 1988. "We're Gonna Make It." The
Godfather of Gospel. Performed by Myrna Sumners.
https://www.invubu.com

*Chapter 7*

Johnson, Jon. "How long you can live without water."
www.medicalnewstoday.com. May 14, 2019

Barrell, Amanda. "How long can you survive without
food?"www.medicalnewstoday.com. March 17, 2020

*Chapter 8*

Preato, Daniel. "Junia, a Female Apostle: An Examination
of the Historical Record." April 26, 2019.
https://www.cbeinternational.org/resource/junia-female-apo
stle-examination-historical-record/

*www.eunicewoodscohee.com*

*https://www.eunicewoodscoheeministries.com*

*Pastoreun22@gmail.com*

*P.O. Box 140341*

*Austin, Texas 78714*

*MeGriHam@gmail.com*

Made in the USA
Columbia, SC
29 September 2023

23592469R00072